THE TRUTH ABOUT MONEY

THE TRUTH ABOUT MONEY

James L. Jordan, PhD, PhD
Deovina N. Jordan, PhD, MD

Copyright Page

Title: THE TRUTH ABOUT MONEY

Paperback ISBN-13: 978-1-64752-030-4
EBook ISBN-13: 978-1-64752-031-1

Copyright, Legal Notice, and Disclaimer

If you have any questions about the content of this book, please contact Deja Jord, Inc.
23811 Washington Avenue, C110, #249
Murrieta, California 92562

Dedication

We dedicate this book to:

All Who Seek The Truth About Money

James L. Jordan, PhD, PhD

and

Deovina N. Jordan, PhD, MD

Prologue

Money is a major influence in how one lives or operates and what one does. This applies to individuals, organizations, governments, and countries. Even religion is dependent upon money and often religious endeavors are focused on gaining money or preventing its loss.

Everyone knows that money exists. However, many people don't know what it really is. For some, money is often regarded as something ethereal. For many, it is viewed as something one has in the bank, namely assets. Hence, at times, people consider it as the measure of a person's "worth." For much of humanity, money is the medium by which one purchases things or pays taxes (e.g., to a governmental body). In addition, money is often seen as being cash. As such, people ask "How much money do you have?" However, money is far more than an asset, a medium, cash, or other forms of financial transaction.

By not knowing what money truly is, or what money really does to people's lives, one has no real idea how to gain mastery over it. If money is considered as something out in the clouds, then it eludes being controlled. As such, money ends up controlling one in ways that persons and even organizations do not truly understand. Therefore, the truth about money must be told. Money must be defined. When one knows what money truly is, then one can understand its power and can free oneself from being its slave. The purpose of this book is to present a new perspective about money by introducing a new definition of money, indicating what it does and explaining why one should control his/ her money.

Jesus Christ told His followers, "The truth shall set you free." He also indicated that no one can serve two masters, money and God. Either one serves God and not money, or one serves money and not God. Therefore, to be able to truly serve God, one has to know money and what it does. In that way, one can live in a manner in which money is not one's master, but one's servant, thereby freeing one to serve God and not money.

To facilitate understanding of the concept of money, what money does, and how to gain mastery over money, the different chapters of this book are presented in two parts (Part 1 and Part 2). The first part features the concepts and theory being presented by the authors. The second part involves excerpts/ quotations made by different individuals that largely concur with the position being taken by the authors of this book. Ownership of the excerpts/ quotations of/ from other authors/ sources is not being claimed by this book's authors. The other authors/ sources are duly noted and their quotes are verifiable via the internet. Utilization of their quotes in Part 2 of the 32 chapters and in Appendix 1 is in accordance with fair use under the United States Copyright Law. As such, the quotes are included only to give support, via historical sources, of the original materials presented in Part 1 of the 32 chapters. The original materials are owned and copyrighted by the authors (James L. Jordan and Deovina N. Jordan) and has been registered as being so by the United States Copyright office.

Much of what applies to an economy as a whole (e.g., debt) can be readily applied to the financial health of individuals. As such, this is not a book about what form of money and how much money to save, or where and when to invest money, or even the differences among occupations (e.g., comparative worth). Such considerations can only take place when one understands what money truly is and what money actually does/ represents. Actual application of such knowledge is up to the individual according to his/ her opportunities, challenges, and economic, social, political, legal, and religious environments.

Table Of Contents

Chapter 1 (Part 1): What Is Money Anyway (According To Standard Definitions)?

Before one can truly address what money is, one has to look at what are some of the existing definitions of money. They are:

"Something generally accepted as a medium of exchange, a measure of value, or a means of payment" (https://www.merriam-webster.com/dictionary/money)

Money is defined in the Business Dictionary as being "anything of value that serves as a (1) generally accepted medium of financial exchange, (2) legal tender for repayment of debt, (3) standard of value, (4) unit of accounting measure, and (5) means to save or store purchasing power." (http://www.businessdictionary.com/definition/money).

Money has also been defined as being: "noun, plural mon·eys, mon·ies. (1) any circulating medium of exchange, including coins, paper money, and demand deposits; (2) paper money;

(3) gold, silver, or other metal in pieces of convenient form stamped by public authority and issued as a medium of exchange and measure of value; (4) any article or substance used as a medium of exchange, measure of wealth, or means of payment, as checks on demand deposit or cowrie." (https://www.dictionary.com/browse/money).

"Money is an economic unit that functions as a generally recognized medium of exchange for transactional purposes in an economy." (https://www.investopedia.com/terms/money).

"Money is any good that is widely used and accepted in transactions involving the transfer of goods and services from one person to another. Economists differentiate among three different types of money: commodity money, fiat money, and bank money. Commodity money is a good whose value serves as the value of money. … Fiat money is a good, the value of which is less than the value it represents as money. … Bank money consists of the book credit that banks extend to their depositors." (https://www.cliffsnotes.com/study-guides/economics/money-and-banking/definition-of-money)

Chapter 1 (Part2): What Is Money Anyway (According To Standard Definitions)? – Relevant Quotes (Quotes

"Every human being who reaches the age of understanding of the purpose of money, wishes for it. Wishing will not bring riches. But desiring riches with a state of mind that becomes an obsession, then planning definite ways and means to acquire riches, and backing those plans with persistence which does not recognize failure, will bring riches." — Napoleon Hill (Think and Grow Rich)

"The definition of money as the sublime good--because it can be turned into all other goods--results in the depreciation of all values that do not pay. What is moral is what returns a profit and satisfies the judgment of the bottom line. Freedom comes to be defined, in practice if not in commencement speeches, as the freedom to exploit. This commercial reading of the text of human natures gives rise to a system that puts a premium on crime, encourages the placid acquiescence in the dishonest thought or deal, sustains the routine hypocrisy of politics and proclaims as inviolate the economic savagery otherwise known as the free market or freedom under capitalism. It is no accident that in a society that presumes a norm of violence, whether on the football field or in the conduct of its business, people speak of deals as 'killings.'" — Lewis Lapham

"Money, it is conventional to argue, is a medium of exchange, which has the advantage of eliminating inefficiencies of barter; a unit of account, which facilitates valuation and calculation; and a store of value, which allows economic transactions to be conducted over long periods as well as geographical distances. To perform all these functions optimally, money has to be available, affordable, durable, fungible, portable and reliable." — Niall Ferguson (The Ascent of Money: A Financial History of the World)

"Though I speak with the tongues of men and of angels, and have not money, I am become as a sounding brass, or a tinkling cymbal. And though I have the gift of prophecy, and understand all mysteries, and all knowledge; and though I have all faith, so that I could remove mountains, and have not money, I am nothing. And though I bestow all my goods to feed the poor, and though I give my body to be burned, and have not money, it profiteth me nothing. Money suffereth long, and is kind; money envieth not; money vaunteth not itself, is not puffed up, doth not behave unseemly, seeketh not her own, is not easily provoked, thinketh no evil; rejoiceth not in iniquity, but rejoiceth in the truth; beareth all things, believeth all things, hopeth all things, endureth all things. . . . And now abideth faith, hope, money, these three; but the greatest of these is money. I Corinthians xiii (adapted)." — George Orwell (Keep the Aspidistra Flying)

Chapter 2: Why A New Definition Of Money Is So Important

Money is not wealth in itself; it only functions in the transactions of that which is wealth. It is a medium of financial exchange. To do so, money has legal backing; else, it would not be legal tender. Money also serves as a measure of value. The point is that money must represent a form of ownership. One does not transact, exchange, or measure the value of that which is not owned. For example, one can exchange food, but no one has yet developed a system to transact, exchange, or measure the value of the gold contained in all celestial bodies in the galaxy except that from earth . It may be in the celestial bodies in great abundance. But, it is not available for transactions and it is not really owned yet by anyone. Indeed, one cannot sell what cannot be bought and one cannot buy that which cannot be sold. This brings us to the next section, namely a new definition of money.

Historically, money was backed by a commodity such as gold or silver. But, money in transactions is most often fiat money (not backed by commodities per se) or bank money (based on credit made by banks). But, since money indicates a transaction of a form of wealth, what is that wealth being exchanged with/ for? Answering that question will enable one to better understand what money is, what money does, and how to best manage money.

Chapter 3 (Part 1): A New Definition of Money

Money is a legal claim of ownership over the goods and services of a person or a people. People who exchange money, sell it, or purchase it, are involved in the acquisition of ownership rights of the goods or services of a person or people. Such a claim can take the form of legal documents (such as currency notes). Because money involves legal ownership claims of goods and services that must be produced by people, the commodity backing money is actually people. As such, money directly influences what people do, what people own and how they behave, along with their freedoms and lives, both in the present and in the future.

Money is not just a piece of paper (or cloth); those represent legal documents of a claim over goods and services. Moreover, money is not simply a medium of exchange since barter can also perform as a medium of exchange, albeit awkwardly and only to a limited scale. Such a definition of money does not address what is actually being exchanged or appropriated. To define money, one must first determine what has value and what is actually being transacted (bought and sold). The answer is direct. What is sold or bought are goods and services. The goods do not have to be manufactured in the present; even gold mined a thousand years ago still has value as gold. A famous painting is still given a valuation and may be bought and sold. It is still a good. Services are not limited to physical labor. For example, services can also entail the information generated by computers and the processes performed by robots. Those services (e.g., the computer, robot) are still owned by someone and are bought and sold using the medium of money.

To better understand the scope of the new definition of money, the components of the definition also have to be addressed. A legal claim of ownership is an enforceable right to demand or assert ownership. Ownership is to have an exclusive right and control over something (in this case the goods and services) of a certain population/ people. Goods refer to tangible items (e.g., objects, products, property) and services refer to activities (e.g., labor, non-physical). For the purposes of money, goods/ property includes land and other non-consumable items and any material of value. Even the organs that comprise one's body can be regarded as a good; they can be assigned an economic value and be bought and sold. Moreover, even one's life is subject to having an economic value placed on it; this is noted in the development of life insurance and other insurances. As such, life is also an economic good. For the purposes of money, services include labor which has been monetized (or its value allocated). As a consequence, knowledge may be viewed as a good (it can be owned in the form of copyrights and patents) and education is a service. Food may be regarded as a good while cooking and preparing food is a service. But the prepared food, the result of the combination of a good and a service, may then be sold in a package (e.g., cans) and then be viewed as a good. In terms of one's organs, the organs themselves are goods while the removal and transplantation of these organs are services. As such, goods and services becomes everything that can be given an economic value, bought and sold, and transferred economically from one party to another. Consequently, goods and services are not limited to human activities. Rain, for example, can be given an economic value and, as a consequence, can be subject to taxation, and its use (as water) can be bought, sold, and controlled. In other words, what God may give freely, people can buy and sell, and governments can tax and control.

Chapter 3 (Part 2): A New Definition Of Money – Relevant Quotes (Quotes from other authors are excluded from the copyright of this book.)

"Economists sometimes distinguish between three types of goods: private goods, which can be purchased by individuals through the market; club goods, which can only be purchased by a group through some organization like a corporation; and public goods, which can only be purchased by whole communities through the state. This is a very helpful terminological distinction, but it should not be allowed to obscure one very important point. As the example of security guards shows, in many cases the good that is purchased is identical; it's just that the way it is purchased differs. Rich people pay their security guards personally. Condo owners pay fees to a condo association, which then pays security guards. Citizens pay taxes to the state, which then pays the police. Exactly the same economic transaction is taking place, but it is organized in a different way. So if you ask whether security should be a private good, a club good, or a public good, the answer will be - it depends. Sometimes it is more efficient to deliver security services through the market; sometimes it will be more efficient to deliver them through the state. From the standpoint of society, the goal should be to choose the delivery system that works best in each case." — Joseph Heath (Efficient Society)

"Financial transactions have displaced the production of goods or services as the source of private fortunes, distorting the value we place upon different kinds of economic activity." — Tony Judt (Ill Fares The Land: A Treatise On Our Present Discontents)

Chapter 4 (Part 1): So Is Money Evil?

A popular passage in the Bible (1 Timothy 6:10, King James Version) states that, "For the love of money is the root of all evil: which while some coveted after, they have erred from the faith, and pierced themselves through with." But, is the money itself evil? That depends. But, one has to first look carefully at the quote. The quote does not say money is evil. It says the love of money is evil. And that love being mentioned is a love for money that takes precedence over love for God and His truth. It emphasizes what Jesus Christ said earlier with "No man can serve two masters: for either he will hate the one, and love the other, or else he will hold to the one, and despise the other. Ye cannot serve God and mammon [money]" (Matthew 6:24, King James Version). Some have claimed that not having money is the root of evil. That does not contradict what was said either by Jesus Christ or by Paul. One can love and serve what one does not have. And, as this book will emphasize, money can become one's master. One has to recognize how money can enslave a person and destroy not only his/ her quality of life but also one's relationship with

God and the rest of humanity. The Bible (Revelation 18:13, King James Version) even mentions the buying and selling of the "souls of men." To buy and sell someone's soul means that one is not only monetizing the souls and lives of persons but also using them in commercial transactions. That appears to be a very good definition of slavery at its ultimate.

The very fact that money represents a legal claim over the goods and services (whatever can be owned) of a people lends itself to abuse. Those who have money control others, what they have, and what they do. Those who do not have money are controlled by others and, as such, are impoverished/ separated from having or doing what they want. As a result, the quality of life diminishes for the impoverished.

In essence, money denotes control. Monetary (economic) control ultimately becomes political/ social control. Whoever controls money controls the people/ society. And whoever controls the money determines what kind of society people will live in. Let's take a look at different political structures that control people and how money is involved.

Communism means control by a party, in the name of the good of the people and based on Karl Marx's political theory, communism ends up primarily benefiting those at the head of the communist party. Under communism, property is publicly owned, with each person working according to their abilities and needs. But this political structure fails to recognize that those who control others often claim to have greater needs and, therefore, have a greater claim on the public wealth. As such, communist regimes often end up becoming dictatorial states.

Socialism, in contrast to communism, is not centered upon Karl Marx's political theory (who saw socialism as being a transitional social state between the downfall of capitalism and communism). Socialism does, however, focus on ownership and regulation of production, distribution, and exchange being under the control of the community as a whole. As such, under socialism, the community as a whole exerts an ownership claim over goods and services and, therefore, money. Socialism also does not take into account that some people, namely those who control the community, also control the money.

Fascism is control of society, in the name of the nation's welfare, by those who control the largest sources of goods and services. With fascism, a particular group of people (e.g., race, nationality) has control over resources above (or at the cost of) the individual. Those who lose the control of their wealth, it turns out, are not those with the greatest wealth or those who are in charge of the government, but those with the least amount of wealth.

Capitalism involves an economic and political system that is controlled by private owners who operate to increase their profit (amount of wealth). Since they, not the state, control the economic and political system, they also control society and politics. Strictly speaking, the corruption of a few, which diminishes the wealth of many, is a capitalistic venture, maximizing the profit margin of the few, even in economic/ political entities that oppose capitalism (e.g., communism).

The common theme is that the minority benefit from the control of the majority. For the majority to control the wealth, democracy would have to be implemented. But, even with a democracy, some become the leaders and their focus ultimately becomes centered on themselves and favoring whoever most supports their own economic and political agenda. As such, one could say democracies vote democracy out of office. As for the majority, regardless of the economic or political system, their ownership of money is proportionally much lower than that richest segment of society. As for the poor, not only do they have few resources to control, their value becomes centered on their services. These tend to be at low cost because the poor compete with the poor regarding the remaining assets under their control, thereby driving down their economic value. That trend is also coupled by the fact that the poor often have debt which diminishes their actual wealth (to be discussed later in the book). Consequently, as for the poor, it comes down to who controls them. It is not a matter of being controlled, but on who controls this segment of society. In terms of those who exert economic control, have the money (are rich), poor lives don't matter. In fact, poor lives are simply another commodity, regardless of the economic/ political system in effect, to be bought and sold by those who own/ control the money. In that sense, money often becomes an evil. Simply replacing/ overthrowing a regime does not change this issue. The new rulers often become like the old rulers. After all, control (power) is addictive and money provides control (power). As such, politics can be encapsulated as being the art of controlling money and the art of controlling money leads to the art of controlling people.

As indicated, whoever controls money, controls people who seek money. Whoever controls all money, controls humanity itself. This is also mentioned in the Bible (Revelation 13:17, King James Version) which states, "No one may be able buy, or to sell, except he who is having the mark, or the name of the beast, or the number of his name." Such predicts a time when all money and, as such, all legal claims of ownership are possessed by a single entity, thereby ending all individual freedoms. How this can happen is intrinsic to the nature of money (legal ownership over goods and services of a people) and is apparent from the implications of that ownership detailed later in this book.

Note that money itself is not evil. Money is neither good nor evil. Money is actually only a tool of commerce. It is how things are monetized and how money is applied that determines whether or not it contributes to good or evil. This book will address how money can be used in both contexts.

Chapter 4 (Part 2): So Is Money Evil? – Relevant Quotes (Quotes from other authors are excluded from the copyright of this book.)

"The lack of money is the root of all evil." — Mark Twain

"So you think that money is the root of all evil? [...] Have you ever asked what is the root of money? Money is a tool of exchange, which can't exist unless there are goods produced and men able to produce them. Money is the material shape of the principle that men who wish to deal with one another must deal by trade and give value for value. Money is not the tool of the moochers, who claim your product by tears, or of the looters, who take it from you by force. Money is made possible only by the men who produce. Is this what you consider evil?" — Ayn Rand (Atlas Shrugged)

"People are wrong when they think that an unemployed man only worries about losing his wages; on the contrary, an illiterate man, with the work habit in his bones, needs work even more than he needs money. An educated man can put up with enforced idleness, which is one of the worst evils of poverty. But a man like Paddy, with no means of filling up time, is as miserable out of work as a dog on the chain. That is why it is such nonsense to pretend that those who have 'come down in the world' are to be pitied above all others. The man who really merits pity is the man who has been down from the start, and faces poverty with a blank, resourceless mind." — George Orwell (Down and Out in Paris and London)

"Money doesn't mind if we say it's evil; it goes from strength to strength. It's a fiction, an addiction, and a tacit conspiracy." — Martin Amis (Money)

“Now I don’t see anything evil in a desire to make money. But money is only a means to some end. If a man wants it for a personal purpose - to invest in his industry, to create, to study, to travel, to enjoy luxury – he’s completely moral. But the men who place money first go much beyond that. Personal luxury is a limited endeavor. What they want is ostentation: to show, to stun, to entertain, to impress others… at the price of their own self-respect. In the realm of greatest importance - the realm of values, of judgment, of spirit, of thought - they place others above self, in the exact manner which altruism demands. A truly selfish man cannot be affected by the approval of others. He doesn’t need it.” — Ayn Rand (The Fountainhead)

“What he realised, and more clearly as time went on, was that money-worship has been elevated into a religion. Perhaps it is the only real religion-the only felt religion-that is left to us. Money is what God used to be. Good and evil have no meaning any longer except failure and success. Hence the profoundly significant phrase, to make good. The decalogue has been reduced to two commandments: one for the employers - the elect, the money priesthood as it were - ‘Thou shalt make money’; the other for the employed - the slaves and underlings - ‘Thou shalt not lose thy job.’” — George Orwell (Keep the Aspidistra Flying)

Chapter 5 (Part 1): Money Facilitates Transactions

Money has value in permitting transactions to be more complicated than that associated with bartering of goods and or services. As a medium of exchange, it can be traded independently of the goods and or services being bought or sold. One does not have to trade a given amount of grain directly for a given amount of bread. One can also use money as a basis for establishing the creation of value being added to goods. For example, steel can have increased value when it is used to make ships, cars, appliances, and other manufactured goods. But, even then, the increased value of a good, having been transformed into another good, still remains a component of the goods and services upon which money derives its value. Money serves as a medium for facilitating the process, but that does not make money the process. Having discussed that, although money can be traded independently, it does not make money independent of the basis of value for the money. Even though the supply of money, and therefore its price, is influenced by private entities involved in the creation and the distribution (allocation) of money, money still has to have some basis for having value. And, even though money is associated with the performance of markets and economies, money itself does not function as the natural basis for markets and economies. People often forget that for a transaction to occur, something must be transacted. While governments can create fiat money (money in the form of notes/ currency), that does not provide the actual value to the goods and services of an economy. Without a foundation which has actual value (goods and services), fiat money (money not supported by ownership/ backing of precious metals) has been produced by governments, often in greater and greater amounts, with resulting decreased worth of that fiat money.

Chapter 5 (Part 2): Money Facilitates Transactions – Relevant Quotes (Quotes from other authors are excluded from the copyright of this book.)

"So much barbarism, however, still remains in the transactions of most civilized nations, that almost all independent countries choose to assert their nationality by having, to their inconvenience and that of their neighbors, a peculiar currency of their own." — John Stuart Mill

"Money speaks sense in a language all nations understand." — Aphra Behn

"Exchange is truly voluntary only when nearly equivalent alternatives exist. Monopoly implies the absence of alternatives and thereby inhibits effective freedom of exchange." — Milton Friedman (Capitalism and Freedom)

"In the whole history of the world, there is but one thing that money cannot buy...to wit--the wag of a dog's tail." — Josh Billings

"If the financial system has a defect, it is that it reflects and magnifies what we human beings are like. Money amplifies our tendency to overreact, to swing from exuberance when things are going well to deep depression when they go wrong. Booms and busts are products, at root, of our emotional volatility." — Niall Ferguson

"By contrast, people who do not trust one another will end up cooperating only under a system of formal rules and regulations, which have to be negotiated, agreed to, litigated, and enforced, sometimes by coercive means. This legal apparatus, serving as a substitute for trust, entails what economists call 'transaction costs.' Widespread distrust in a society, in other words, imposes a kind of tax on all forms of economic activity, a tax that high-trust societies do not have to pay." — Francis Fukuyama (Trust: Human Nature and the Reconstitution of Social Order)

"What is missing in our economic system is a central value that can encompass everything that can be transacted and used to assign the proper relative value to everything." — Ilchi Lee (Change: Realizing Your Greatest Potential)

"A free economy is an economy run by free beings. And free beings are responsible beings. Economic transactions in a regime of private property depend not only on distinguishing mine from yours, but also on relating me to you. Without accountability, nobody is to be trusted, and without trust, the virtues that are attributed to the free economy would not arise." — Roger Scruton (How to Be a Conservative)

Chapter 6 (Part 1): Monetary Transference Without Consent

Economic theories treat money as a means to promote transactions; such transactions are treated as largely being voluntary among/ between participants. But, money is not dependent upon how it is acquired. The transference of legal ownership claims to what one owns is often not voluntary. Examples often cited in economics papers include inflation, taxation, and debt. But, the transactions go far beyond that. Theft can mean the acquisition of an ownership claim from one party to another. Not all theft is illegal. Theft can come in the form of taxation and inflation; both of these will be addressed in greater detail later in this book. Theft can also occur outside of legal procedures. Examples of these are burglary, larceny, petty theft, grand theft, and embezzlement. Even corruption falls under the category of being a kind of theft.

Theft is often indicated as the loss of an amount of money (or object(s) which is/ are monetized as having a particular value/s). This, in effect, separates the object and the ownership of it from what the owner had to do, have, or trade in order to obtain it. If the original owner had to provide labor and save the proceeds thereof to purchase something, then the theft actually represents a seizure of that part of the owner's life and time used to perform the necessary labor. Since even reimbursements for theft (if they occur) have deductibles and tax deductions, then that part of the monetary value not compensated for represents a non-recoverable loss. To regain the equivalency of what was lost, then the affected party/ parties must earn or surrender legal rights to the ownership of other goods and services.

Theft is also often depicted as the seizure of a good. But, the actual possession of a good through theft is not dependent on outright seizure. Theft can also occur as a consequence of deception. The owner may make a fraudulent claim believed by the buyer. But, the value of the claim declared by the seller is less than the value of the good or service sought by the buyer. This has been occurring for centuries as a means to take properties (e.g., land) from another. The difference between the claim and actual value of the good or service is seen as a form of profit. But, since the transaction is based on dishonesty, it is actually a form of theft. The seller of the legal claim is not selling that claim to another based upon truth, but upon a lie. That is also how scams have worked in the past. People are promised a value that will never come to them. The value is instead delivered to the seller of the product. One recent case of this was the subprime loans that made some people wealthy, but many more poor. People even lost their entire savings (representing their total legal claims to possess). This led many to their untimely deaths. But even after these deceivers who have committed theft by fraud have been imprisoned (and considered felons), some kept most of the monies and are still honored by society. Indeed, one can find many reality television shows and even entertainment media (e.g., movies, theater, the internet, books, magazines) glorifying the gaining of wealth through deception and often presented as cunning business. But, theft still means that someone lost claim to part of his/ her life that was necessary to obtain ownership of that which was stolen.

Even if losses from theft are covered by insurance, there is transference of money, namely legal claim to goods and services. Insurance is the pooling of goods and services so that in case of unusual need (e.g., disaster, theft), that pool (built from the contribution of the participants) can be tapped into to help those who were adversely affected. Such claims are often limited to a value less than the actual loss. Hence, even with insurance, the original owner of the money loses some of it. But, from a standpoint of those who purchased insurance, not directly affected by the loss, their goods and services represent the money being transferred to those who suffered a loss. More than that, it is often ineffective coverage of a few by others, since not all the goods and services rendered to purchase the insurance is applied to the remediation of losses. Some of their goods and services are for the benefit (profit) of those overseeing the insurance. The net consequence is that insurance results in a net decrease in overall wealth by those who pool their 'money' – namely goods and services – to help affected members and to sustain/ make rich those who manage the insurance. That loss is further increased when governmental agencies become involved. The government may demand payment (e.g., taxes) to be paid before recovery from a loss can even be attempted. Moreover, the monies paid into insurance are monies already taxed by the government (even when it is not the case for monies paid out by the government), resulting in a further loss of goods and services owned by the participants.

Finally, we come to the ultimate form of theft, namely homicide and murder. Homicide or murder clearly ends the victim's legal claims to anything of this life/ world. One has to be alive to have a legal claim over anything in this life.

Chapter 6 (Part 2): Monetary Transference Without Consent – Relevant Quotes (Quotes from other authors are excluded from the copyright of this book.)

"They look upon fraud as a greater crime than theft, and therefore seldom fail to punish it with death; for they allege, that care and vigilance, with a very common understanding, may preserve a man's goods from thieves, but honesty has no defence against superior cunning; and, since it is necessary that there should be a perpetual intercourse of buying and selling, and dealing upon credit, where fraud is permitted and connived at, or has no law to punish it, the honest dealer is always undone, and the knave gets the advantage." — Jonathan Swift (Gulliver's Travels)

"Just see these superfluous ones! They steal the works of the inventors and the treasures of the wise. Culture, they call their theft - and everything becometh sickness and trouble unto them! Just see these superfluous ones! Sick are they always; they vomit their bile and call it a newspaper. They devour one another, and cannot even digest themselves. Just see these superfluous ones! Wealth they acquire and become poorer thereby. Power they seek for, and above all, the lever of power, much money - these impotent ones!" — Friedrich Nietzsche (Thus Spake Zarathustra: A book for all and none)

"Millions of men perpetrated against one another such innumerable crimes, frauds, treacheries, thefts, forgeries, issues of false money, burglaries, incendiarisms, and murders as in whole centuries are not recorded in the annals of all the law courts of the world, but which those who committed them did not at the time regard as being crimes." — Leo Tolstoy (War and Peace)

"That's the funny thing about stealing money---it always seems to be the rich people who have the most of it." — Ari Marmell (Lost Covenant [Widdershins Adventures, #3])

"Corporate War: The theft of money from the common people by corporate sponsored politicians to fund arguably illegal wars in far off lands." — Steven Magee

"Just as it is impossible to know when a swimming fish is drinking water, so it is impossible to find out when a government servant is stealing money." — Kautilya (The Arthashastra)

"I respect ordinary thieves much more than I respect politicians. Ordinary thieves take my money without pretense. Unlike typical politicians, these thieves don't bore me with silly explanations of why their thievery is for the greater good. Nor do ordinary thieves insult my intelligence by proclaiming that they'll use the money that they steal from me to make my life better than I would have made my life had my money not been swiped from me." — Walter Williams

"Everyone in the room knew about leveraged buyouts, often called LBOs. In an LBO, a small group of senior executives, usually working with a Wall Street partner, proposes to buy its company from public shareholders, using massive amounts of borrowed money. Critics of this procedure called it stealing the company from its owners and fretted that the growing mountain of corporate debt was hindering America's ability to compete abroad. Everyone knew LBOs meant deep cuts in research and every other imaginable budget, all sacrificed to pay off debt. Proponents insisted that companies forced to meet steep debt payments grew lean and mean. On one thing they all agreed: The executives who launched LBOs got filthy rich." — Bryan Burrough (Barbarians at the Gate: The Fall of RJR Nabisco)

Chapter 7 (Part 1): A History Of Money – Before Money And The Advent Of Money

Many economies in the distant past, along with some primitive economies in recent times, did not utilize money. Barter was the manner by which products and labor were exchanged. Such economies had the features of being small and involved transactions with only few things. But, bartering is not consistent in exchanges and is limited as to what can be traded and with whom transactions can be conducted.

In time, transactions involved the use of primitive forms of money. The most marketable commodity being exchanged became the medium of exchange, thereby functioning as money. For example, shells have been used as money. This reached an extreme in the Pacific islands of Yap (part of Micronesia) where ownership of large doughnut-shapes rocks were utilized as money. Other economies used gold or silver as money. And, even such items as receipts of tobacco were used as a form of money in the American colonies (due to hard currency being in short supply) and bottles (or cases of rum) were used as money in the early British West Africa colonial era. Even as recently as the Second World War, prisoners of war used cigarettes from Red Cross packages as money.

Note: Money no longer represents the most marketable commodity being exchanged. That is because money is not backed by any particular commodity and it is not constructed from anything that has, in itself, a marketable value. As such, money has become to be something different than it had been at its origin. Money currently represents a legal claim of ownership, including that of marketable commodities.

Chapter 7 (Part 2): A History Of Money – Before Money And The Advent Of Money – Relevant Quotes (Quotes from other authors are excluded from the copyright of this book.)

"Before our white brothers arrived to make us civilized men, we didn't have any kind of prison. Because of this, we didn't have any delinquents. Without a prison, there can't be no delinquents. We had no locks nor keys; therefore, among us

there were no thieves. When someone was so poor that he couldn't afford a horse, a tent or a blanket, he would, in that case, receive it all as a gift. We were too uncivilized to give great importance to private property. We didn't know any kind of money and, consequently, the value of a human being was not determined by his wealth. We had no written laws laid down, no lawyers, no politicians; therefore, we were not able to cheat and swindle one another. We were really in bad shape before the white man arrived and I don't know how to explain how we were able to manage without these fundamental things that (so they tell us) are so necessary for a civilized society."
— John Fire Lame Deer

"The definitive anthropological work on barter, by Caroline Humphrey of Cambridge, could not be more definitive in its conclusions: 'No example of a barter economy, pure and simple, has ever been described, let alone the emergence from it of money; all available ethnography suggests that there never has been such a thing.'" — David Graeber (Debt - Updated and Expanded: The First 5,000 Years)

"Nobody ever saw a dog make a fair and deliberate exchange of one bone for another with another dog. Nobody ever saw one animal by its gestures and natural cries signify to another, this is mine, that is yours; I am willing to give this for that....But man has almost constant occasion for the help of his brethren, and it is in vain for him to expect it from their benevolence only. He will be more likely to prevail if he can interest their self-love in his favour, and show them that it is for their own advantage to do for him what he requires of them. Whoever offers to another a bargain of any kind, proposes to do this. Give me that which I want, and you shall have this which you want, is the meaning of every such offer; and it is in this manner that we obtain from one another the far greater part of those good offices which we stand in need of." — Adam Smith (An Inquiry into the Nature and Causes of the Wealth of Nations)

"Do you wish to know whether that day is coming? Watch money. Money is the barometer of a society's virtue. When you see that trading is done, not by consent, but by compulsion - when you see that in order to produce, you need to obtain permission from men who produce nothing - when you see that money is flowing to those who deal, not in goods, but in favors - when you see that men get richer by graft and by pull than by work, and your laws don't protect you against them, but protect them against you - when you see corruption being rewarded and honesty becoming a self-sacrifice - you may know that your society is doomed. Money is so noble a medium that it does not compete with guns and it does not make terms with brutality. It will not permit a country to survive as half-property, half-loot. "Whenever destroyers appear among men, they start by destroying money, for money is men's protection and the base of a moral existence. Destroyers seize gold and leave to its owners a counterfeit pile of paper. This kills all objective standards and delivers men into the arbitrary power of an arbitrary setter of values. Gold was an objective value, an equivalent of wealth produced. Paper is a mortgage on wealth that does not exist, backed by a gun aimed at those who are expected to produce it. Paper is a check drawn by legal looters upon an account which is not theirs: upon the virtue of the victims. Watch for the day when it bounces, marked:

'Account overdrawn.' "When you have made evil the means of survival, do not expect men to remain good. Do not expect them to stay moral and lose their lives for the purpose of becoming the fodder of the immoral. Do not expect them to produce, when production is punished and looting rewarded. Do not ask, 'Who is destroying the world?' You are." — Ayn Rand (Atlas Shrugged)

Chapter 8 (Part 1): A History Of Money – Gold

The concept of money was historically linked to gold. The possession of gold was deemed to constitute a nation's wealth. The supply and demand for gold became the foundation of wealth. Such a thought about money, termed bullionism, dominated European courts until the end of the sixteenth century. The initial bullionists were administrators of the sovereign's private finances. The result was a household economy. To maintain that economy, precious metal outflow from a nation was restricted.

Gold can function contrary to the growth of an economy since it interferes with valuation (pricing) of goods being traded. Gold becomes a bottleneck. Goods and services end up depending on gold (which is seen as having value) and not in their actual value to a society. But, gold itself produces nothing. Moreover, it is often hoarded, at which time it does nothing to increase wealth or to increase the production of either goods or services.

In actuality, gold is not money. It is simply another commodity. But, it is a commodity that is useful for barter. Because of its limited quantity, it is also useful as it limits the amount of money in circulation (thereby, limiting the tendency of governments to print increasingly worthless currency). When government officials remove money production from a limiting factor (e.g., gold), they often seek to increase the money supply by simply printing more of it. The danger behind this trend was noted by John Maynard Keynes who wrote, "By a continuing process of inflation, governments can confiscate, secretly and unobserved, an important part of the wealth of their citizens." The cumulative effects of inflation have been noted in the United States. The Investor's Business Daily reported in 2013 that "you could buy six times more stuff [in 1960] than you can buy today." That means money saved in 1960 lost five-fifths of its value due to inflation; that value had been stolen from the citizens. And, where did that wealth go? Inflation has been seen as a means by government to pay off its debts by using cheaper currency to pay off the debt of more expensive currency. But, many people are simply left with the cheaper currency and increased poverty. Their goods and services were stolen by inflation and an increased supply of money. Inflation becomes a means by which not only wealth is transferred from the many to the few, but also a means by which government exercises its control over the goods and services of its people. This use of inflation was particularly acute in other countries, such as Latin America and Eastern Europe, where annual inflation reached four digit levels.

When gold is seen as the measure of valuation, then the transactions for goods and services are first defined by bartering to of gold to sell or buy a good or a service. The essential component of the transaction is not the bartering of gold, it still remains the selling or buying of goods and services. Gold only serves as a medium for such transactions. Yet, gold, being heavy and requiring storage and transport, does not readily lend itself to large financial transactions. For example, if a corporation were to purchase another corporation for billions in currency, moving a large volume of gold would not be feasible. Rather, a contract indicating a transaction is more feasible. That is where money, not in the form of gold, helps expedite transactions of goods and services.

Chapter 8 (Part 2): A History Of Money – Gold – Relevant Quotes (Quotes from other authors are excluded from the copyright of this book.)

"We have gold because we cannot trust governments." — Herbert Hoover

"If more of us valued food and cheer and song above hoarded gold, it would be a merrier world." — J.R.R. Tolkien

"Chains of gold are still chains."— Robert Their (Storm and Silence)

"We will answer their demand for a gold standard by saying to them: 'You shall not press down upon the brow of labor this crown of thorns, you shall not crucify mankind upon a cross of gold.'" — William Jennings Bryan

"All the codes of ethics they'll try to ram down your throat are just so much paper money put out by swindlers to fleece people of their virtues. The code of competence is the only system of morality that's on a gold standard." — Ayn Rand (Atlas Shrugged)

"More gold had been mined from the mind of men than the earth itself." — Napoleon Hill (Think and Grow Rich: The Landmark Bestseller Now Revised and Updated for the 21st Century)

"The gold standard was incapable of preventing the sort of financial booms and busts that were, and continue to be, such a feature of the economic landscape. These bubbles and crises seem to be deep-rooted in human nature and inherent to the capitalist system. By one count, there have been sixty different crises since the early seventeenth century - the first documented bank panic can, however, be dated to A.D. 33 when the Emperor Tiberius had to inject one million gold pieces of public money into the Roman financial system to keep it from collapsing." — Liaquat Ahamed (Lords of Finance: The Bankers Who Broke the World)

"In the absence of the gold standard, there is no way to protect savings from confiscation through inflation. There is no safe store of value." — Alan Greenspan

"Points 1 and 2. The United States represents less than 5 percent of the world's population; it consumes more than 25 percent of the world's resources. This is accomplished to a large degree through the exploitation of other countries, primarily in the developing world. Point 3. The United States maintains the largest and most sophisticated military in the world. Although this empire has been built primarily through economics - by EHMs - world leaders understand that whenever other measures fail, the military will step in, as it did in Iraq. Point 4. The English language and American culture dominate the world. Points 5 and 6. Although the United States does not tax countries directly, and the dollar has not replaced other currencies in local markets, the corporatocracy does impose a subtle global tax and the dollar is in fact the standard currency for world commerce. This process began at the end of World War II when the gold standard was modified; dollars could no longer be converted by individuals, only by governments. During the 1950s and 1960s, credit purchases were made abroad to finance America's growing consumerism, the Korean and Vietnam Wars, and Lyndon B. Johnson's Great Society. When foreign businessmen tried to buy goods and services back from the United States, they found that inflation had reduced the value of their dollars - in effect, they paid an indirect tax. Their governments demanded debt settlements in gold. On August 15, 1971, the Nixon administration refused and dropped the gold standard altogether." — John Perkins (The Secret History of the American Empire: The Truth About Economic Hit Men, Jackals, and How to Change the World)

Chapter 9 (Part 1): Monetary Theories – Knut Wicksell

Knut Wicksell (1898) addressed money from the standpoint of interest rates and price level changes. At that time, gold was no longer the basis for the volume of money in circulation. Instead, most payments in modern financial transactions occur via transfers among bank accounts. The bank accounts usually develop when banks extend loans to borrowers and permit them to have deposits in corresponding amounts. The result is the occurrence of expenditures and income; these are in turn transferred to the sellers of goods and labor (services). Those who sell goods and labor (services) then deposit funds into the banks as savings. The savings are then utilized to extend additional loans by which to finance production of goods. The banks earn a nominal interest on the difference between the interest rates paid to depositors and received from lenders. The interest earned is variable due to differences in the claims to current goods and future goods. But, it is important (in terms of money defined in this book) that a definite association exists between money, the value of money, and goods (both present and future).

Chapter 9 (Part 2): Monetary Theories – Knut Wicksell – Relevant Quotes (Quotes from other authors are excluded from the copyright of this book.)

"[Capitalism assumed] that from the beginning, all men are equal. If that were so, everyone would be equipped with the same working power, the same education and, above all, the same economic assets … each person would [then] have only himself to blame if he did not succeed." — Knut Wicksell

"A bank is a place that will lend you money if you can prove that you don't need it." — Bob Hope

"What begins as a banking crisis ends with a banking crisis, even if it goes through the states' accounts." — Mark Blyth (Austerity: The History of a Dangerous Idea)

"The Federal Reserve dictated not only the interest rates at which banks could borrow from one another, as it does today, but also the interest rates that banks could pay on savings accounts." — Yaron Brook (Free Market Revolution: How Ayn Rand's Ideas Can End Big Government)

Chapter 10 (Part 1): Monetary Theories – Irving Fisher

Irving Fisher (1911) was important in establishing a functional relationship between the price level and the volume of money. He had already presented (in 1896) that the nominal interest of money and the rate of inflation approximates the real rate of interest. In other words, interest rates adjust to changes in inflation. If that were not the case, financial investors would not make loans that do not protect their real income. This is important (in terms of money defined in this book) in that money in circulation can increase when goods and services also increase in value. But, in addition, it also means that increasing money, without an increased value in goods and services, contributes to inflation. Still, when applied to the definition of money (as presented earlier in this book), money is shown as being strongly associated with a legal claim on goods and services.

Chapter 10 (Part 2): Monetary Theories – Irving Fisher – Relevant Quotes (Quotes from Irving Fisher are excluded from the copyright of this book.)

"As a matter of fact, what investment can we find which offers real fixity or certainty of income? ... As every reader of this book will clearly see, the man or woman who invests in bonds is speculating in the general level of prices, or the purchasing power of money." — Irving Fisher

"A bond price, for example, will grow with accrued interest between two coupon cuttings. That growth in its value is not income but increase of capital. Only when the coupon is detached does the bond render, or give off, a service, and so yield income. The income consists in the event of such off-giving the yielding or separation, to use the language of the United States Supreme Court. If the coupon thus given off is reinvested in another bond, that event is outgo, and offsets the simultaneous income realized from the first bond. There is then no net income from the group but only growth of capital. If the final large payment of the principal is commonly thought of not as income (which it is if not reinvested) but as capital, it is because it is usually and normally so reinvested." — Irving Fisher (The Theory of Interest)

Chapter 11 (Part 1): Monetary Theories – John Maynard Keynes

Keynes, primarily active during the great depression years (1930s), made the assumption that adjustments in supply to demand occur in a short time frame. As such, employment is based more on total demand than upon structural details of supply-side adjustments. As such, aggregate income transforms into expenditures, resulting in saving equals investment. But, in terms of the definition for money in this book, what is the demand for, if not for goods and services?

Chapter 11 (Part 2): Monetary Theories – John Maynard Keynes – Relevant Quotes (Quotes from other authors are

excluded from the copyright of this book.)

"A sound banker is not one who foresees danger and avoids it," wrote John Maynard Keynes, "but one who, when he is ruined, is ruined in a conventional way along with his fellows, so that no one can really blame him." — Anonymous

"The ideas of economists and political philosophers, both when they are right and when they are wrong, are more powerful than is commonly understood. Indeed, the world is ruled by little else. Practical men, who believe themselves to be quite exempt from any intellectual influences, are usually slaves of some defunct economist." — John Maynard Keynes

"If you owe your bank a hundred pounds, you have a problem. But if you owe a million, it has." — John Maynard Keynes

"Capitalism is the astounding belief that the most wickedest of men will do the most wickedest of things for the greatest good of everyone." — John Maynard Keynes

"Capitalism is the extraordinary belief that the nastiest of men for the nastiest of motives will somehow work together for the benefit of all." — John Maynard Keynes

"When the accumulation of wealth is no longer of high social importance, there will be great changes in the code of morals. We shall be able to rid ourselves of many of the pseudo-moral principles which have hag-ridden us for two hundred years, by which we have exalted some of the most distasteful of human qualities into the position of the highest virtues. We shall be able to afford to dare to assess the money-motive at its true value. The love of money as a possession - as distinguished from the love of money as a means to the enjoyments and realities of life - will be recognized for what it is, a somewhat disgusting morbidity, one of those semi-criminal, semi-pathological propensities which one hands over with a shudder to the specialists in mental disease." — John Maynard Keynes (Economic Possibilities for Our Grandchildren)

"There is a danger of expecting the results of the future to be predicted from the past." — John Maynard Keynes

"Once we allow ourselves to be disobedient to the test of an accountant's profit, we have begun to change our civilization. 'Ancient Egypt was doubly fortunate, and doubtless owed to this its fabled wealth, in that it possessed two activities, namely, pyramid-building as well as the search for the precious metals, the fruits of which, since they could not serve the needs of man by being consumed, did not stale with abundance. The Middle Ages built cathedrals and sang dirges. Two pyramids, two masses for the dead, are twice as good as one; but not so two railways from London to York. Thus we are so sensible, have schooled ourselves to so close a semblance of prudent financiers, taking careful thought before we add to the 'financial' burdens of posterity by building them houses to live in, that we have no such easy escape from the sufferings of unemployment. We have to accept them as an inevitable result of applying to the conduct of the State the maxims which are best calculated to 'enrich' an individual by enabling him to pile up claims to enjoyment which he does not intend to exercise at any definite time." — John Maynard Keynes (The General Theory of Employment, Interest, and Money)

"Keynes was a great economist. In every discipline, progress comes from people who make hypotheses, most of which turn out to be wrong, but all of which ultimately point to the right answer. Now Keynes, in The General Theory of Employment, Interest and Money, set forth a hypothesis which was a beautiful one, and it really altered the shape of economics. But it turned out that it was a wrong hypothesis. That doesn't mean that he wasn't a great man!" — Milton Friedman

Chapter 12 (Part 1): Monetary Theories – Milton Friedman

According to Friedman, the demand for money is determined by two factors. The first is the rate of inflation. The second is the effect of money on the holding of other assets. Central banks have a primary task in the economic environment of keeping money growth proportionately and timely in association with the production potential of an economy. In terms of the definition for money in this book, what is the production potential of an economy if it is not directly linked to the production of goods and services?

Chapter 12 (Part 2): Monetary Theories – Milton Friedman – Relevant Quotes (Quotes from Milton Friedman are

excluded from the copyright of this book.)

"One of the great mistakes is to judge policies and programs by their intentions rather than their results." — Milton Friedman

"The great virtue of a free market system is that it does not care what color people are; it does not care what their religion is; it only cares whether they can produce something you want to buy. It is the most effective system we have discovered to enable people who hate one another to deal with one another and help one another." — Milton Friedman

"Government has three primary functions. It should provide for military defense of the nation. It should enforce contracts between individuals. It should protect citizens from crimes against themselves or their property. When government-- in pursuit of good intentions tries to rearrange the economy, legislate morality, or help special interests, the cost come in inefficiency, lack of motivation, and loss of freedom. Government should be a referee, not an active player." — Milton Friedman

"Nothing is so permanent as a temporary government program." — Milton Friedman

“Underlying most arguments against the free market is a lack of belief in freedom itself.” — Milton Friedman

“The key insight of Adam Smith’s Wealth of Nations is misleadingly simple: if an exchange between two parties is voluntary, it will not take place unless both believe they will benefit from it. Most economic fallacies derive from the neglect of this simple insight, from the tendency to assume that there is a fixed pie, that one party can gain only at the expense of another.” — Milton Friedman

“Only people have incomes and they derive them through the market from the resources they own, whether these be in the form of corporate stock, or of bonds, or of land, or of their personal capacity.” — Milton Friedman (Free to Choose: A Personal Statement)

“Nobody spends somebody else’s money as carefully as he spends his own. Nobody uses somebody else’s resources as carefully as he uses his own. So if you want efficiency and effectiveness, if you want knowledge to be properly utilized, you have to do it through the means of private property.” — Milton Friedman

“When the law interferes with people’s pursuit of their own values, they will try to find a way around. They will evade the law, they will break the law, or they will leave the country. Few of us believe in a moral code that justifies forcing people to give up much of what they produce to finance payments to persons they do not know for purposes they may not approve of. When the law contradicts what most people regard as moral and proper, they will break the law - whether the law is enacted in the name of a noble ideal such as equality or in the naked interest of one group at the expense of another. Only fear of punishment, not a sense of justice and morality, will lead people to obey the law." — Milton Friedman (Free to Choose: A Personal Statement)

"Every country, it always is and must be the interest of the great body of the people to buy whatever they want of those who sell it cheapest. The proposition is so very manifest, that it seems ridiculous to take any pains to prove it; nor could it ever have been called in question, had not the interested sophistry of merchants and manufacturers confounded the common sense of mankind. Their interest is, in this respect, directly opposite to that of the great body of the people." — Milton Friedman (Free to Choose: A Personal Statement)

"It is ironic that the Great Depression was produced by government but was blamed on the private enterprise system. The Federal Reserve System explained in its 1933 annual report how much worse things would have been if the Federal Reserve had not behaved so well, yet the Federal Reserve was the chief culprit in making the depression as deep as it was. So the government produced the depression, the private enterprise system got blamed for it, and there was a tremendous change in attitudes." — Milton Friedman (Why Government Is the Problem)

"If you put the government in charge of the Sahara Desert, in five years there'd be a shortage of sand." — Milton Friedman

“President Kennedy said, ‘Ask not what your country can do for you - ask what you can do for your country.’…Neither half of that statement expresses a relation between the citizen and his government that is worthy of the ideals of free men in a free society. ‘What your country can do for you’ implies that the government is the patron, the citizen the ward. ‘What you can do for your country’ assumes that the government is the master, the citizen the servant.” — Milton Friedman (Capitalism and Freedom)

“A society that puts equality - in the sense of equality of outcome - ahead of freedom will end up with neither equality nor freedom. The use of force to achieve equality will destroy freedom, and the force, introduced for good purposes, will end up in the hands of people who use it to promote their own interests.” — Milton Friedman (Free to Choose: A Personal Statement)

“The only person who can truly persuade you is yourself. You must turn the issues over in your mind at leisure, consider the many arguments, let them simmer, and after a long time, turn your preferences into convictions.” — Milton Friedman

Chapter 13 (Part 1): An Evolution Of Money – The Non-Gold Economy

Money is no longer backed by gold, but by the 'full faith and credit of the national government.' We will return to this statement shortly. But, money remains a unit of measurement for financial/ economic transactions. When supply and demand is constant, and the money in circulation does not change, then the value of goods and services also remain stable. This is facilitated by the money being portable, with excepted value and function for payment for goods and services. Money, in that sense, also becomes the medium for taxation. A problem arises when the money supply increases without a corresponding increase in goods and services. For a while, the economy may appear to be stimulated. That is because the true value of the goods and services has not yet caught up to the actual amount of money. But when it does, the stimulatory effect ends, actual wealth has been redistributed, and the costs of goods and services cost more in monetary terms. The fact remains that the goods and services have not increased in actual value, but the money used to facilitate their transaction has decreased in value. This is a component of why 'the rich get richer and the poor get poorer.' This process of wealth transfer is abetted by the tax system. When goods and services increase in price, while the value of money decreases, the tax system still operates as if the value of money remains unchanged. As such, taxation increases regarding the wealth of those with less real money, decreasing their ownership of goods and services being transferred with the medium of money.

In contrast to increasing the monetary supply, governments can also decrease the supply of currency (money). That can actually cause a negative effect on the economy. Less currency pursuing a given amount of goods and services increases the value of those goods and services. The numbers of transactions decrease because of the value of the 'money' increasing. As such, the production of goods and services can decrease because of the decrease in financial transactions.

Chapter 13 (Part 2): An Evolution Of Money – The Non-Gold Economy – Relevant Quotes (Quotes from other authors are excluded from the copyright of this book.)

“Paper money has had the effect in your state that it will ever have, to ruin commerce, oppress the honest, and open the door to every species of fraud and injustice.” — George Washington

“If the State uses this power systematically in order to force the community to accept a particular sort of money whose employment it desires for reasons of monetary policy, then it is actually carrying through a measure of monetary policy. The States which completed the transition to a gold standard a generation ago, did so from motives of monetary policy. They gave up the silver standard or the credit-money standard because they recognized that the behaviour of the value of silver or of credit money was unsuited to the economic policy they were following.” — Ludwig von Mises (The Theory of Money and Credit)

“Only government can take perfectly good paper, cover it with perfectly good ink and make the combination worthless.” — Milton Friedman

“The instant that any government obtains a monetary printing press, it becomes a deeply dishonest government, empowered to rob people by stealth, a government with the power to print money knows no limits.” — Jeffrey Tucker

“Rather than justice for all, we are evolving into a system of justice for those who can afford it. We have banks that are not only too big to fail, but too big to be held accountable.” — Joseph E. Stiglitz

"In short, there is no question that a country can run a stable paper currency without a gold standard, a central bank, a lender of last resort, or much regulation; and not only avoid disaster, but perform well. Bottom-up monetary systems – known as free banking – have a far better track record than top-down ones. Walter Bagehot, the great nineteenth-century theorist of central banking, admitted as much. In his influential book Lombard Street, he effectively conceded that the only reason a central bank needed to be a lender of last resort was because of the instability introduced by the existence of a central bank." — Matt Ridley (The Evolution of Everything: How New Ideas Emerge)

"A system of capitalism presumes sound money, not fiat money, manipulated by a central bank. Capitalism cherishes voluntary contracts and interest rates that are determined by savings, not credit creation by a central bank." — Ron Paul

"Roughly two fifths of the world's population is effectively outside the financial system, without access to bank accounts, much less credit." — Niall Ferguson (The Ascent of Money: A Financial History of the World)

"Gold standard - which the United States had dropped in 1933 - Ever since, the Treasury had been printing money freely to finance first the New Deal and now the war. Howard feared that someday the United States might wind up like Germany in the 1920s, when people had to cart wheelbarrows of money down the street to buy a head of cabbage - the direct result of Germany being forced to deplete its gold stock to pay reparations after World War I. The economic chaos that resulted was one of the major factors that had led to Hitler." — Alice Schroeder (The Snowball: Warren Buffett and the Business of Life)

Chapter 14 (Part 1): Full Faith And Credit Of The National Government

This brings us back to the phrase 'full faith and credit of the national government.' From an economic standpoint, it refers to the government's full borrowing power (no matter what its borrowing) as a promise to repay in a timely manner. In order to do so, it issues debt securities supported via taxes, borrowing, and other revenue sources. As such, full faith and credit of the national government is a statement of power over the people it governs.

Let us look at the clause - full faith and credit - from the definition of money as being a legal claim over ownership of goods and services. First, money is a legal tender. As such, it is a legal document to the ownership of something. The 'full faith and credit of the national government' also indicates that ownership is by the government. The government uses money, as a legal document, to claim ownership over the goods and services of its people.

To uphold its claim of 'full faith and credit,' the national government does not need to have large reserves of gold. The reserves of gold claimed by the government are those owned by the people under its jurisdiction. If the government needs gold to back its currency, it simply has to take it from the people it controls. As such, the 'full faith and credit of the national government' is actually a legal proclamation that it has the power to tax and to appropriate to itself whatever it wants for its own purposes. It also establishes the power of the government to enforce the use of its currency for 'all debts public and private.' As such, fiat money becomes the basis of the government's claim over all the goods produced and services provided by its people and all transactions involving such.

The government, consequently, does not merely own all goods and services; it can take them from its people at its own discretion and for its own purposes. That includes all transactions involving goods and services, no matter how private they may be. Because of that, the government actually owns everything. Since services are also involved, whatever a person does can be taxed and controlled. And, because the government owns services, it also ends up owning the people who provide those services. That is why the government can enforce people to work to pay off the taxes it imposes upon the people. It can do so because it owns the people. And, what the government owns, it also controls. 'Full faith and credit of the national government' enshrines this into law. Whatever the government borrows, the people under its jurisdiction are obligated to pay.

Chapter 14 (Part 2): Full Faith And Credit Of The National Government – Relevant Quotes (Quotes from other authors are excluded from the copyright of this book.)

"When the people find that they can vote themselves money, that will herald the end of the republic." — Benjamin Franklin

"The American Republic will endure until the day Congress discovers that it can bribe the public with the public's money." — Alexis de Tocqueville

"I see in the near future a crisis approaching that unnerves me and causes me to tremble for the safety of my country. . . . corporations have been enthroned and an era of corruption in high places will follow, and the money power of the country will endeavor to prolong its reign by working upon the prejudices of the people until all wealth is aggregated in a few hands and the Republic is destroyed." — Abraham Lincoln

"The US Federal Reserve, Bank of England, Bank of Japan, and European Central Bank (for the 12 euro currency countries) have powers beyond what most people imagine. As a result, they and the Bank of International Settlements (BIS) control financial conditions everywhere in an increasingly borderless world where significant economic events in one nation affect others for better or worse. Based in Basle, Switzerland, BIS is the central banker for central bankers, a banking boss of bosses accountable to no government. Moreover, it's privately owned by its members, the most powerful ones having most influence. Along with dominant central banks, financial elitists established it to control world economies globally, ideally with a single currency." — Stephen Lendman (How Wall Street Fleeces America: Privatized Banking, Government Collusion and Class War)

"Behind the troubled banks and the increasingly troubled insurance agencies stands 'the full faith and credit' of the Government - in effect, a promise, sure to be honored by Congress, that all citizens will chip in through taxes or through inflation to make all depositors whole." — G. Edward Griffin (The Creature from Jekyll Island)

Chapter 15 (Part 1): Debt

Debt is defined as the amount of money borrowed by one party from another party. As such, debt is often a legal obligation. Debt results from current income being less than current spending. Debt can arise from one's own imbalanced income and spending. It can also result from being obligated to pay for the imbalance of income and spending of another party. This arises when the citizenry are obligated to pay off the debts of their nation.

Debt is the result of an excess amount of claims made on goods and/ or services such that one party in a monetary transaction is stressed or unlikely to pay it off in current goods/ services. Debt can be temporary with the claims being liquid (able to be covered) by current goods/ services. When the debt cannot be covered by current monies (legal claims on goods and services), such has to be paid with future claims on goods and services. Debt can be personal in that it represents an individual's inability to satisfy transference of ownership in the present and/ or future. To cover such debt, one is obligated to transfer what ownership rights he has in future goods/ services.

Government debt is placed upon the people that are under a government's jurisdiction. The government debt is covered by the seizing of future ownership claims that the people it controls/ governs possesses in the present or will possess in the future. In essence, government debt is paid by transferring its debt upon those people in its jurisdiction. This has major importance regarding taxation and allocation/ expenditure of monies/ wealth by the government.

Chapter 15 (Part 2): Debt – Relevant Quotes (Quotes from other authors are excluded from the copyright of this book.)

"[A man] finds himself forced by necessity to borrow money. He knows that he will not be able to repay it, but sees also that nothing will be lent to him unless he promises stoutly to repay it in definite time. He desires to make this promise, but he has still so much conscience as to ask himself: Is it not unlawful and inconsistent with duty to get out of a difficulty in this way?

Suppose, however, that he resolves to do so, then the maxim of his action would be expressed thus: When I think myself in want of money, I will borrow money and promise to repay it, although I know that I never can do so. Now this principle of self-love or of one's own advantage may perhaps be consistent with my whole future welfare; but the question now is, Is it right? I change then the suggestion of self-love into a universal law, and state the question thus: How would it be if my maxim were a universal law? Then I see at once that it could never hold as a universal law of nature, but would necessarily contradict itself. For supposing it to be a universal law that everyone, when he thinks himself in a difficulty, should be able to promise whatever he pleases, with the purpose of not keeping his promise, the promise itself would become impossible, as well as the end that one might have in view in it, since no one would consider that anything was promised to him, but would ridicule all such statements as vain pretenses." — Immanuel Kant (Fundamental Principles of the Metaphysic of Morals)

"A man in debt is so far a slave." — Ralph Waldo Emerson

"Money dignifies what is frivolous if unpaid for." — Virginia Woolf (A Room of One's Own)

"We don't have a trillion-dollar debt because we haven't taxed enough; we have a trillion-dollar debt because we spend too much." — Ronald Reagan

Chapter 16 (Part 1): The Rise Of The Debt Economy

Many persons are in debt. Governments are in debt. In fact, the debt of the world far exceeds the value of the goods and services available in the world. So, what is debt? Debt is a promise/ legal obligation to pay off something obtained in the present by selling rights to what will develop in the future. As such, debt involves the selling of current wealth at the cost of future production/ possessions/ work and, therefore, future freedoms. Because debt involves the selling of the future, the ability to control the future is also lost. That in combination with accumulating interest rates means not only a loss of freedom (thereby economic slavery), but also a decline of ownership of goods and services by the many to be owned by the few. For a while, the accumulation of debt may appear to stimulate the economy. But, that is only a temporary stimulus at best. In reality, debt is the transference of wealth, thereby increasing overall poverty and government control. After all, if the government owns everything now, debt means that it will own everything in perpetuity.

The debt economy has also introduced money in a manner distinct from circulating currency. It has introduced the widespread use of credit cards, debit cards, and checks. This causes a major dissociation between value, money, and what is really being transacted. The money being transacted is viewed as not money, but the ramifications of the transaction are still those of a monetary-based exchange. By causing a dissociation of the transaction from money, a number of things happen. First, buyers tend to buy more and get into debt or deeper in debt. Second, since all transactions entail the formation of a data base, all transactions can be evaluated and controlled by a third party (e.g., banks, government). That gives greater power to third party control over economic transactions. And, third, it gives feedback to the seller who can better target those to whom to sell, thereby affecting the price of items being sold. In the end, people are transferring ownership of their goods and services without being truly aware that they are doing so. They are engaged in legal claims of ownership without even knowing such claims are being administered. Finally, it serves to increase the monetary supply. The true rate of inflation is no longer subject just to the amount of currency in circulation. It is also a function of the number of transactions occurring and the value of such transactions. In essence, it becomes a high-tech form of barter, but with the fact that money is not readily visible as a component of the transaction. But, money is still involved; albeit, in a less obvious format.

The debt economy, since it involves transference of legal claims/ rights over future goods and services, means that persons (and nations) are selling their futures. But, once a person transfers ownership over his/ her goods or services, present and/ or future, that legal claim of ownership can be bought and sold just like any other commodity. The person becomes another object of trade. In fact, because of the debt economy, even life has become a commercial commodity. For that which is owned by someone else is controlled by someone else. When what one does in life is sold, such as with labor, that becomes the possession of whoever purchases it. In the end, that which is bought with debt in the present can be at the cost of enslavement tomorrow.

The same holds true for nations. Once a nation surrenders its goods and services to another nation, or even to a group of persons (e.g., banks, individuals, international organizations), it ceases, as a matter of fact, to be a truly sovereign nation. The nation simply becomes a source of income for a third party and its citizens suffer as a consequence. In reality, under the worldwide debt economy, nations have become commodities which may be bought and sold.

One problem many persons and even nations face is how to finance a debt. The problem becomes particularly acute when interest is used to pay interest. Since the principal remains unpaid, the repurchase of goods and services remains in the hands of a third party. Another problem occurs when debt is incurred to pay debt. When that happens, the debt becomes a commodity (a kind of property) that can also be bought and sold. The claim of ownership over goods and services becomes more complicated as the layers of debt have to be paid off before the principal can even be addressed. Debt increases. But, ownership disperses among a number of owners or becomes concentrated in the hands of a few.

Chapter 16 (Part 2): The Rise Of The Debt Economy – Relevant Quotes (Quotes from other authors are excluded from the copyright of this book.)

"Money is a great servant but a bad master." — Francis Bacon

"Don't think money does everything or you are going to end up doing everything for money." — Voltaire

"It is incumbent on every generation to pay its own debts as it goes - a principle which, if acted on, would save one-half the wars of the world." — Thomas Jefferson

"Americans used to be 'citizens.' Now we are 'consumers.'" — Vicki Robin (Your Money or Your Life)

"Consumer debt is the lifeblood of our economy. All modern nation-states are built on deficit spending. Debt has come to be the central issue of international politics. But nobody seems to know exactly what it is, or how to think about it. The very fact that we don't know what debt is, the very flexibility of the concept, is the basis of its power. If history shows anything, it is that there's no better way to justify relations founded on violence, to make such relations seem moral, than by reframing them in the language of debt- above all, because it immediately makes it seem that it's the victim who's doing something wrong. Mafiosi understand this. So do the commanders of conquering armies. For thousands of years, violent men have been able to tell their victims that these victims owe them something. If nothing else, they 'owe them their lives' (a telling phrase) because they haven't been killed." — David Graeber

[illegible]

Chapter 17 (Part 1): Taxation

Taxation can be best understood when one considers what constitutes money. Money represents a legal claim on goods and services by one group (who possesses the claim) upon another group (who does not possess the claim but provides goods and services). In consideration of money being defined as such, taxation represents a governmental legal claim on the goods or services of a person or persons (persons include organizations and corporations). Hence, taxation is the exercise of the claim of ownership by the government that must be surrendered to the government upon demand. To pay that claim by a government, the government may seize or control present goods and services. It can force people to do labor to settle a claim by the government. As noted in the definitions presented, taxation would be an economic transaction to settle a debt to the government. The debt may not be a debt entered into by the taxpayer but a debt entered into by the government. The government then imposes or transfers the tax burden to the people in its jurisdiction by collecting taxes to pay that debt. Therefore, a debt incurred by the government may be paid for by imposing claims on whatever future goods and services that its people may have or produce or generate or provide.

Taxation on taxation represents a form of a compound claim to increase a claim on wealth. Since taxes may be collected by one entity, but that entity is also taxed by another entity, those people paying taxes to the first entity are forced to acquiesce to both taxes by surrendering claims to assets, goods or services which are not subject to the original focus of either taxing entity. The net result is that the two taxation entities exert their legal claims of ownership on the assets, goods or services of the taxpayers. Since the claims of ownership of the taxpayers' assets, goods of services by the taxation entities increase, the legal claims of ownership by the taxpayers decrease and the monies held by the people being taxed decrease. Taxation increases the power of those who seize wealth to enhance the government's claim to the taxed people's goods and services. One consequence of placing taxes on taxes is that it may become impossible for the present goods and services of a person/ persons to be sufficient to pay both. Taxes that treat taxes as just money are no longer founded on a legal claim of ownership to any particular good or service. And, since taxes do not tend to take other taxes into consideration, the resulting compounded claims can exceed the value of the goods and services being taxed. The benefit to the taxing agencies is that they may claim the taxes being imposed are lower than is actually occurring. But, the impact on the taxpayers is the decrease in their money not represented by the claims being presented about the levels of taxes (due to taxes themselves being taxed).

Chapter 17 (Part 2): Taxation – Relevant Quotes (Quotes from other authors are excluded from the copyright of this book.)

"I am in favor of cutting taxes under any circumstances and for any excuse, for any reason, whenever it's possible." — Milton Friedman

"We must make our choice between economy and liberty or confusion and servitude...If we run into such debts, we must be taxed in our meat and drink, in our necessities and comforts, in our labor and in our amusements...if we can prevent the government from wasting the labor of the people, under the pretense of caring for them, they will be happy."— Thomas Jefferson

"Taxation is just a sophisticated way of demanding money with menaces." — Terry Pratchett (Night Watch [Discworld, #29; City Watch, #6])

"Many people want the government to protect the consumer. A much more urgent problem is to protect the consumer from the government." — Milton Friedman

"The avoidance of taxes is the only intellectual pursuit that carries any reward." — John Maynard Keynes

"Pro-taxation shills complain about the 'need' to steal money in order to support the 'greater good.' What greater good? The shills' good pet projects, of course." — Mike Klepper

"The widespread enthusiasm for reducing government taxes and other impositions is not matched by a comparable enthusiasm for eliminating government programs - except programs that benefit other people." — Milton Friedman (Free to Choose: A Personal Statement)

"A study conducted at Harvard found that Reagan-era tax cuts sparked a mass career switch among the country's brightest minds, from teachers and engineers to bankers and accountants. Whereas in 1970, twice as many male Harvard grads were still opting for a life devoted to research over banking, twenty years later the balance had flipped, with one and a half times as many alumni employed in finance. The upshot is that we've all gotten poorer. For every dollar a bank earns, an estimated equivalent of 60 cents is destroyed elsewhere in the economic chain. Conversely, for every dollar a researcher earns, a value of at least $5 - and often much more - is pumped back into the economy. Higher taxes for top earners would serve, in Harvard science-speak, "to reallocate talented individuals from professions that cause negative externalities to those that cause positive externalities. In plain English: Higher taxes would get more people to do work that's useful." — Rutger Bregman (Utopia for Realists: How We Can Build the Ideal World)

"To simplify, the state steals money – taxes - from parents in order to use that money to kidnap children from those very parents. This is why reform may be impossible, for the very nature of the system is unethical and based on the destruction of others." — Carlos Morales (Legally Kidnapped: The Case Against Child Protective Services)

"The capital resources of the nation are not increased by using the tax collector rather than the stock market to mobilize them." — Milton Friedman (Free to Choose: A Personal Statement)

Chapter 18 (Part 1): Taxation – Types Of Taxes

A claim of ownership by the government over goods and services can take a number of forms; the transference of such a claim to a government or from a government represents a monetary transaction. That is because money is a legal claim of ownership to goods and services. Some of these taxes are briefly addressed in the following.

Estate Tax: In order to be able to transfer legal ownership claim over accumulated goods/ property, some legal rights to ownership, either from the estate or the inheritors, must be delivered to the government.

Income Tax: In order to produce a good or service, some of that good or service must be done for and surrendered to the government. If such a transaction is not done "voluntarily," the government may impose a claim of ownership which may be even greater than the original claim to ownership.

Property Tax: In order to own something (have a claim to it), enforceable by the government, the person who "owns" a taxable property has to provide a good/ service at the demand of the government to maintain such ownership. If such a tax is not paid, then the government may exert a claim of ownership to the property, seize it, and give it to someone else who will provide the government with goods and services in order to exert a claim of ownership over that property. Property taxes transform ownership of the land by the so-called property owner into a relationship of renting said property from the true owner, the government.

Sales Tax: In order to make a claim over a good or service, such transference to another (acquisition by another) can only be performed if the legal claim to some good or service is surrendered to the government.

Chapter 18 (Part 2): Taxation – Types Of Taxes – Relevant Quotes (Quotes from other authors are excluded from the copyright of this book.)

Estate Tax

"Just as income tax returns allow us to study changes in income inequality, estate tax returns enable us to study changes in the inequality of wealth." — Thomas Piketty (Capital in the Twenty-First Century)

"Another argument: The rich are job creators. They are helping the poor. If their taxes are cut, they can create more jobs. Ah, facts again. The rich actually tend to keep their money by buying prime real estate, yachts, art, and the like - things that will appreciate in value without giving back much to the economy as a whole. Moreover, the rich don't just give jobs out of the goodness of their hearts. Look at economics from the perspective of work: Working people are profit-creators. The rich only create jobs when they can get employees who can create profit for them. The poor create profit for the rich. Conservatives" — George Lakoff (Moral Politics: How Liberals and Conservatives Think, Third Edition)

"When you get rid of the estate tax," he (Warren Buffett) said, "you're basically handing over command of the country's resources to people who didn't earn it. It's like choosing the 2020 Olympic team by picking the children of all the winners at the 2000 Games." — Barack Obama

"It was expected that a proper burgher would leave from a third to a half of his movable property for uses that would benefit the public and his own estate in the next world. Now the state takes over such functions by means of inheritance taxes. The judgment of the state is substituted for that of the decedent, and the merit of voluntary well-doing is lost." — Morris Bishop (The Middle Ages)

"Everyone's an equal shareholder. Birth shares are inalienable, and death duties are unavoidable. The estate tax is one hundred per cent. In between, you can buy and sell and earn as much as you like." — Ken MacLeod (Dissidence)

"Already, data showed that the American dream of rags to riches, the Horatio Alger story, was largely a myth. Economic mobility was extremely limited. The abolition of the estate tax could solidify these changes, creating a new 'class' society, based not on ancient nobility as in Europe, but on the bonanza of the Roaring Nineties." — Joseph E. Stiglitz (The Roaring Nineties: A New History of the World's Most Prosperous Decade)

Income Tax

"When there is an income tax, the just man will pay more and the unjust less on the same amount of income." — Plato

"The freedoms won by Americans in 1776 were lost in the revolution of 1913." — Frank Chodorov (The Income Tax: Root of All Evil)

"1913 wasn't a very good year. 1913 gave us the income tax, the 16th amendment and the IRS." — Ron Paul

"The income tax has made more liars out of the American people than golf has." — Will Rogers

"Income tax returns are the most imaginative fiction being written today." — Herman Wouk

"The hardest thing in the world to understand is the income tax." — Albert Einstein

"There is no worse tyranny than to force a man to pay for what he does not want merely because you think it would be good for him." — Robert A. Heinlein (The Moon is a Harsh Mistress)

"The government spenders tell us, for example, that if the national income is $1,500 billion then federal taxes of $360 billion a year would mean that only 24 percent of the national income is being transferred from private purposes to public purposes. This is to talk as if the country were the same sort of unit of pooled resources as a huge corporation, and as if all that were involved were a mere bookkeeping transaction. The government spenders forget that they are taking the money from A in order to pay it to B. Or rather, they know this very well; but while they dilate upon all the benefits of the process to B, and all the wonderful things he will have which he would not have had if the money had not been transferred to him, they forget the effects of the transaction on A. B is seen; A is forgotten." — Henry Hazlitt (Economics in One Lesson: The Shortest and Surest Way to Understand Basic Economics)

"One thing is clear: The Founding Fathers never intended a nation where citizens would pay nearly half of everything they earn to the government." — Ron Paul

“Because the state uses violence to achieve its ends, and there is no rational end to the use of violence, states grow until they destroy civilized interactions through the corruption of money, contracts, honesty, family, and self-reliance. No state in history has ever been contained. It’s only taken a little more than a century for the US - founded on the idea of limited government, to break the bonds of the constitution, institute the income tax, take control of the money supply and the educational system and begin its catastrophic expansion.” — Stefan Molyneux

“Once you realize that trickle-down economics does not work, you will see the excessive tax cuts for the rich as what they are - a simple upward redistribution of income, rather than a way to make all of us richer, as we were told.” — Ha-Joon Chang (23 Things They Don’t Tell You about Capitalism)

“The only beneficiaries of income taxation are the politicians, for it not only gives them the means by which they can increase their emoluments but it also enables them to improve their importance. The have-nots who support the politicians in the demand for income taxation do so only because they hate the haves; although they delude themselves with the thought that they might get some of the pelt. The fact is that the taxing of incomes cannot in any way improve their economic condition.” — Frank Chodorov (Income Tax: The Root of All Evil)

“When the government is able to collect tax and seize private property without just compensation, it is an indication that the public is ripe for surrender and is consenting to enslavement and legal encroachment. A good and easily quantified indicator of harvest time is the number of public citizens who pay income tax despite an obvious lack of reciprocal or honest service from the government." — David Icke (The Perception Deception - Part One)

"Whether he knows it or not, the middle-income American is taxed as though he were living in a socialist society." — Gore Vidal (Selected Essays)

"Paradoxical as it may seem, the evolution of our income tax has been from a low-rate tax relying for revenue on the high income group to a high-rate tax relying on the middle and lower-middle income groups." — John Brooks (Business Adventures: Twelve Classic Tales from the World of Wall Street)

"When personal incomes are taxed 50, 60 or 70 percent, people begin to ask themselves why they should work six, eight or nine months of the entire year for the government, and only six, four or three months for themselves and their families. If they lose the whole dollar when they lose, but can keep only a fraction of it when they win, they decide that it is foolish to take risks with their capital." — Henry Hazlitt (Economics in One Lesson: The Shortest and Surest Way to Understand Basic Economics)

"All told, over the period 1932-1980, nearly half a century, the top federal income tax rate in the United States averaged 81 percent." — Thomas Piketty (Capital in the Twenty-First Century)

Property Tax

"The fact that Trump paid no tax came to light when casino regulators issued a public report on his fitness to own a casino. Trump's tax returns showed negative income. That's because Congress lets big real estate investors offset their income from salaries, stock market gains, consulting fees, and other income with losses from depreciation in the value of their buildings. If these paper losses for the declining value of their buildings are greater than their cash income from other sources, real estate investors can legally tell the IRS that their income is less than zero and no federal income tax is due." — David Cay Johnston (The Making of Donald Trump)

Chapter 19 (Part 1): Non-Taxation Forms Of Government Revenue

Not every tax is termed as a tax, but the end result is that some good or service must be rendered/ surrendered to the government to have ownership of some good or service. Some of these may be court/ legal fees, building fees, professional license fees, and usage fees. Note: There are more non-taxation sources of government revenue than are listed here.

Court fees: In order to exert one's legal right to a given good or service, a good or service must also be transferred to the court.

Building permits/ fees: In order to build on one's own land, one has to provide a good or service to the government. This also tends to increase the level of property tax on the affected property. The use of permits also affirms that the true ownership of property belongs to the government.

Professional license fees: In order to earn an income (get a claim over a good or a service), one has to surrender part of the claim to one's good or service to the government.

Usage fees: In order to use one's or another's property, one has to surrender a good or a service to the government. Toll roads are an example. Taxes may be collected to build a road, but to use the road one has to transfer more claims of ownership to the government.

Chapter 20 (Part 1): Inflation – An Alternative To Taxation

Inflation is defined as being a general rise in prices. With inflation, each unit of money progressively purchases a smaller legal claim on goods and services. Simply put, the demand for goods and services is greater than the supply at a given price. Because bidding for those goods and services continues (due to demand), the prices to purchase such goods and services rise accordingly.

Inflation has been termed as being a creation of greater and greater amounts of money. But, that is not completely precise. Inflation involves an increase in currency which, by definition, represents an increase in legal claims of ownership over an established amount of goods and services. When the number of claims increases in an economy, the relative proportion of each claim diminishes relative to a given unit of good or service. Because inflation represents a greater supply of money, and fiat money only takes the use of a printer to manufacture, inflation has been used as a means for governments to pay off their debt burdens without having to resort to higher taxes. The raising of taxes may bring upon resistance, even open rebellion, against a government.

Inflation has a particularly adverse effect on savings. Those who save see the loss of their proportion of legal claim to goods and services. That loss of purchasing power becomes claims of ownership that are effectively transferred to the government. As such, inflation becomes a hidden tax, particularly on the poor. The rich can avoid some of the impact of inflation by maintaining their claims of ownership in real estate, stocks, and other tangible assets. Such assets increase in price with inflation. But, the poor do not have such inflation-resistant assets and, as such, their true wealth gets taken away by the government with its hidden and broad tax which is inflation. The government may seek to alleviate the problem with domestic programs but that actually only increases the domestic expenditures or debt and, ultimately, poverty.

In the long run, the government can steal everything from a population using inflation. An example is that of Weimer Germany. In July 1920, 40 marks were worth one American dollar. By November 1923, more than 4 trillion marks were worth one American dollar. Savings were demolished. Goods became unaffordable. Fewer purchases were made. Production of new goods declined. The economy collapsed. But the printing presses kept turning out currency, albeit worthless. A similar story has been told elsewhere, such as in Latin America in 1990 and in Venezuela currently.

Chapter 20 (Part 2): Inflation – An Alternative To Taxation – Relevant Quotes (Quotes from other authors are excluded from the copyright of this book.)

"Inflation is taxation without representation." — Milton Friedman

"These coins are not very valuable. Jack went out to get a napoleon changed, so as to have money suited to the general cheapness of things, and came back and said he had 'swamped the bank, had bought eleven quarts of coin, and the head of the firm had gone on the street to negotiate for the balance of the change.' I bought nearly half a pint of their money for a shilling myself. I am not proud on account of having so much money, though. I care nothing for wealth." — Mark Twain (The Innocents Abroad)

"Inflation is the one form of taxation that can be imposed without legislation." — Milton Friedman

"There is no record of a prolonged war or a great social upheaval which has not been accompanied by a change in the legal tender, but an almost unbroken chronicle in every country which has a history, back to the earliest dawn of economic record, of a progressive deterioration in the real value of the successive legal tenders which have represented money." — John Maynard Keynes

"On the contrary, the inflation itself is partly a response to the reaction. As it has become politically less attractive to vote higher taxes to pay for higher spending, legislators have resorted to financing spending through inflation, a hidden tax that can be imposed without having been voted, taxation without representation. That is no more popular in the twentieth century than it was in the eighteenth." — Milton Friedman (Free to Choose: A Personal Statement)

"Inflation is always and everywhere a monetary phenomenon." — Milton Friedman (Money Mischief: Episodes in Monetary History)

"The first people to get the new money are the counterfeiters, which they use to buy various goods and services. The second receivers of the new money are the retailers who sell those goods to the counterfeiters. And on and on, the new money ripples out through the system, going from one pocket or till to another. As it does so, there is an immediate redistribution effect. For first, the counterfeiters, then the retailers, etc. have new money and monetary income they use to bid up goods and services, increasing their demand and raising the prices of the goods that they purchase. But as prices of goods begin to rise in response to the higher quantity of money, those who haven't yet received the new money find the prices of the goods they buy have gone up, while their own selling prices or incomes have not risen. In short, the early receivers of the new money in this market chain of events gain at the expense of those who receive the money toward the end of the chain, and still worse losers are the people (e.g., those on fixed incomes such as annuities, interests, or pensions) who never receive the new money at all." — Murray N. Rothbard

"Inflation is caused by too much money chasing after too few goods." — Milton Friedman

"I was reading in the paper today that Congress wants to replace the dollar bill with a coin. They've already done it. It's called a nickel." — Jay Leno

"Five simple truths embody most of what we know about inflation: Inflation is a monetary phenomenon arising from a more rapid increase in the quantity of money than in output (though, of course, the reasons for the increase in money may be various). In today's world, government determines - or can determine - the quantity of money. There is only one cure for inflation: a slower rate of increase in the quantity of money. It takes time - measured in years, not months - for inflation to develop; it takes time for inflation to be cured. Unpleasant side effects of the cure are unavoidable." — Milton Friedman (Free to Choose: A Personal Statement)

"Consistently and uninterruptedly, continued inflation must eventually lead to collapse. The purchasing power of money will fall lower and lower, until it eventually disappears altogether. It is true that an endless process of depredation can be imagined. We can imagine the purchasing power of money getting continually lower without ever disappearing altogether, and prices getting continually higher without it ever becoming impossible to obtain commodities in exchange for notes. Eventually, this would lead to a situation in which even retail transactions were in terms of millions and billions and even higher figures; but the monetary system itself would remain. But such an imaginary state of affairs is hardly within the bounds of possibility. In the long run, a money which continually fell in value would have no commercial utility. It could not be used as a standard of deferred payments. For all transactions in which commodities or services were not exchanged for cash, another medium would have to be sought. In fact, a money that is continually depreciating becomes useless even for cash transactions. Everybody attempts to minimize his cash reserves, which are a source of continual loss." — Ludwig von Mises (The Theory of Money and Credit)

"One reason inflation is so destructive is because some people benefit greatly while other people suffer; society is divided into winners and losers. The winners regard the good things that happen to them as the natural result of their own foresight, prudence, and initiative. They regard the bad things, the rise in the prices of the things they buy, as produced by forces outside their control. Almost everyone will say that he is against inflation; what he generally means is that he is against the bad things that have happened to him." — Milton Friedman (Free to Choose: A Personal Statement)

Chapter 21 (Part 1): Inflation – Banks, A Non-Government Source

Inflation has historically been linked to the overproduction of currency by the national government. But, are the claims of ownership (termed money) dependent solely upon the governmental issuance of currency? No, banks lend out money at a greater amount than which is actually held by the banks. This is called the multiplier effect. For every unit of currency, the bank may lend out the equivalent of 5, 10, 20 or even more than that, in terms of loans, than is actually existent in currency. Banks often seek to have the least amount of currency holdings, particularly during times of prosperity. By doing so, they can reap the rewards of having profits in accordance with a larger base (monies earning monies). This can backfire when the economy is less prosperous. The needed funds held by a bank can then become insufficient to back the loans made out. In such a case, the bank may go bankrupt, have to be bailed out by the government, and/ or seize assets of its creditors (depositors).

The net effect of banks / financial institutions lending out far in excess of their reserves is that the economy behaves in a manner consistent with the working money in circulation, not the actual currency in circulation. For example, if a bank places ten units of currency value into circulation, via loans, the economy behaves just the same as if the government had released ten times the original value of currency in circulation. After all, money is a legal claim to ownership over goods and services. Does it matter if such a legal claim arises from an action of the bank or from the action of a national government? If someone does not return a yield on the loan from a bank, the corresponding collateral may be seized by the bank. Such is the case with foreclosures.

The government is complacent with this arrangement. After all, if claims over goods and services increase, the government can partake in the increased reported value of goods and services. For example, if the price of housing goes up, even if the amount of real currency does not increase, property taxes increase nevertheless. In essence, the essential impact on the economy is much the same as if the amount of currency issued by the government actually did increase. But, that burden upon the economy is not shared equally. While the debt is still in place, it is the bank/ financial institution that actually owns the property/ good/ service bought by the money being borrowed. But, the bank/ financial institution does not have to pay the property tax (or other taxes) associated with such ownership. The tax that a private person may end up paying is not associated with actual ownership of a property/ good/ service (since that is owned by another), but on the debt that one has on the property/ good/ service. As such, actual ownership and debt, particularly regarding taxes, have become separated. Even when a property's value becomes less than its purchase value, the taxes on such property are still fixed to the debt/purchase price of that property. On top of that, if one defaults in tax payments, the property may be foreclosed (returned to its actual owner), but the debt not paid by the borrower is still taxed as being income.

Another phenomenon emerges when the perceived money in circulation is greater than actual currency to back it. It is called the monetization of debt. Since debt, via lending at levels greater than actual currency, legal claims of ownership over goods and services are susceptible to being bundled and traded, just as if actual currency was involved. After all, the debt being transacted represents claims of ownership over something material. Such gives rise to even debt being placed on debt, which is then also monetized. The level of debt then increase far beyond the multiplier effect of currency in circulation or loans from financial institutions (e.g., banks). The accumulation of debt into packages, called derivatives, has led to an interesting phenomenon. Since banks and other financial institutions hold so many derivatives, monies deposited with them cease to be the properties of the depositors. The bank owns the monies as being unsecured loans and the first to have claim over such monies are those who hold the derivatives (collections of debts). Such placing debt upon debt, and transacting the result as being money, has a side-effect. There is not enough wealth in the world to cover the Ponzi-like financial arrangement. That being said, not only the present generation is buried in debt, but all generations into the indeterminate future are also buried in debt.

The transfer of bank-induced inflation can have another consequence. When large financial institutions fail or are vulnerable to failure, the government may intervene via bank bailouts. That uses monies collected in taxes and ends up simply being transference of monies (legal claims of ownership) from the taxpayers to the financial institution(s) involved. The taxpayers (and the country as a whole) become poorer, but the banks/ financial institutions prosper. This problem will be addressed later in this book.

Chapter 21 (Part 2): Inflation – Banks, A Non-Government Source – Relevant Quotes (Quotes from other authors are excluded from the copyright of this book.)

"I sincerely believe that banking establishments are more dangerous than standing armies, and that the principle of spending money to be paid by posterity, under the name of funding, is but swindling futurity on a large scale." — Thomas Jefferson

“Banks are allowed to loan $10 for every dollar they actually possess, which means that 90 per cent of all the money in our bank accounts is not covered by actual coins and notes.” — Yuval Noah Harari (Sapiens: A Brief History of Humankind)

“While everyone else must pay their debts or go bankrupt, the banks are permitted to refuse redemption of their receipts, at the same time forcing their own debtors to pay when their loans fall due. The usual name for this is a ‘suspension of specie payments.’ A more accurate name would be ‘license for theft;’ for what else can we call a governmental permission to continue in business without fulfilling one’s contract?” — Murray N. Rothbard (What Has Government Done to Our Money?)

“Bank-friendly writers and lobbyists fostered a myth that the economy needed its investment banks to remain solvent to keep the economy functioning. But many former officials, including Bair, SIGTARP‘s Neil Barofsky, and Reagan Administration budget director David Stockman, rejected the claims that public guarantees for reckless bank loans was needed to protect insured depositors. Retail savings and checking accounts were never threatened by the bad gambles that banks made. But this myth had to be promoted in order for Paulson, Geithner Bernanke and other bank protectors to persuade Congress to overrule Bair and make government (‘taxpayers’) pay. Their aim was to save the banks from being nationalized, and to protect bankers from being prosecuted for fraud or reining in the exorbitant salaries and bonuses they had given themselves. No attempt was made to change the system that had led to the crash.” — Michael Hudson (Killing the

Host: How Financial Parasites and Debt Bondage Destroy the Global Economy)

Chapter 22 (Part 1): The Destruction of Money – War

Nonproductive use of money leads to the destruction of money. Not all money destroyed is destroyed by the government. People destroy money when they indulge in that which they neither need nor want. Religions destroy money when they spend money on that which glorifies a few persons (at the cost of many). In that manner, it has been said that Christian Europe was kept in a state of poverty when cathedral building was valued more than having universities for advanced learning. And, war is one way that government destroys money; every year of war costs as much as three to four years of peace.

War is a unique and peculiar endeavor that has the objective of deliberately destroying goods and services and, as such, money (since it is a legal claim to ownership of such goods and services). Not only are people and properties damaged or destroyed with war, the articles used to wage war are either destroyed in the war (e.g., by bombs) or become obsolescent without any use for increasing society's production of goods and services. That which has been destroyed by war has to be rebuilt after the war. That alone requires the allocation of monies to return or increase the production base of a society. The allocation of monies is actually the transference of claims over goods and services to an endeavor to provide for the production of goods and services decreased by war.

Chapter 22 (Part 2): The Destruction of Money – War – Relevant Quotes (Quotes from other authors are excluded from the copyright of this book.)

"War is a matter not so much of arms as of money."— Thucydides (History of the Peloponnesian War)

"Who wishes to fight must first count the cost."— Sun Tzu (The Art of War)

"Of all the enemies to public liberty, war is, perhaps, the most to be dreaded, because it comprises and develops the germ of every other. War is the parent of armies; from these, proceed debts and taxes; and armies, and debts, and taxes are the known instruments for bringing the many under the domination of the few. In war, too, the discretionary power of the Executive is extended; its influence in dealing out offices, honors, and emoluments is multiplied; and all the means of seducing the minds, are added to those of subduing the force, of the people. The same malignant aspect in republicanism may be traced in the inequality of fortunes, and the opportunities of fraud, growing out of a state of war, and in the degeneracy of manners and of morals engendered by both. No nation could preserve its freedom in the midst of continual warfare." — James Madison (Letters and other writings of James Madison)

"War is Mass Murder, Conscription is Slavery, Taxation is Robbery." — Murray N. Rothbard

"War prosperity is like the prosperity that an earthquake or a plague brings." — Ludwig von Mises (Nation, State, and Economy: Contributions to the Politics and History of Our Time)

"It is in war that the State really comes into its own: swelling in power, in number, in pride, in absolute dominion over the economy and the society." — Murray N. Rothbard

"The military state is the final form to which every planned economy tends rapidly." — Isabel Paterson

"If race or class war divides us into hostile camps, changing political argument into blind hate, one side or the other may overturn the hustlings with the rule of the sword. If our economy of freedom fails to distribute wealth as ably as it has created it, the road to dictatorship will be open to any man who can persuasively promise security to all; and a martial government, under whatever charming phrases, will engulf the democratic world." — Will Durant (The Lessons of History)

"Every gun that is made, every warship launched, every rocket fired signifies, in the final sense, a theft from those who hunger and are not fed, those who are cold and are not clothed. This world in arms is not spending money alone. It is spending the sweat of its laborers, the genius of its scientists, the hopes of its children. The cost of one modern heavy bomber is this: a modern brick school in more than 30 cities. It is two electric power plants, each serving a town of 60,000 population. It is two fine, fully equipped hospitals. It is some fifty miles of concrete pavement. We pay for a single fighter plane with a half million bushels of wheat. We pay for a single destroyer with new homes that could have housed more than 8,000 people. This is, I repeat, the best way of life to be found on the road the world has been taking. This is not a way of life at all, in any true sense. Under the cloud of threatening war, it is humanity hanging from a cross of iron.... Is there no other way the world may live?" — Dwight D. Eisenhower

"It is curious to note that when, for reasons of conscience, people refuse to kill, they are often exempted from active military duty. But there are no exemptions for people who, for reasons of conscience, refuse to financially support the bureaucracy that actually does the killing. Apparently, the state takes money more seriously than life." — Karl Hess

Chapter 23 (Part 1): The Destruction of Money – Prisons

Prisons are a unique structure wherein people are removed from society to reduce their harm, including monetary, upon society at a cost of the allocation of goods and services from the economy without a corresponding increase in production of goods and services. As such, prisons function to reduce the value of money. The reason is that utilization of goods and services, without a corresponding increase in their production, is a form of inflation. Prisons, in essence, impose a demand on goods and services but without any obvious increase in monetary supply. To pay for prisons, society has to increase its monetary supply (which results in inflation), borrow from the present and future (which results in debt), or increase its overall production (to compensate for the costs). The first two options, increased monetary supply and borrowing, are inflationary (inflation was addressed earlier). The latter, an increase in overall production, is often not a factor in deciding expenditures upon prisons.

Prisons not only remove persons from society and place them in nonproductive status (though many of these persons were negatively productive to begin with), they also require that persons in society, including the victims of crimes, surrender their ownership claims to their goods and services to pay for prisons. In fact, because keeping someone in prison is so expensive, the harm of placing a thief, such as for petty crime, easily outweighs the negative costs to society of that person before he/ she went to prison. A consequence is that prison ensures that there are no victimless crimes. That which had been termed as a victimless crime ends with imprisonment. With prison, those who pay for the incarceration become victims. Those who had been victims of crime become victims again. This is so because if they do not pay taxes to support the incarceration of the person(s) who had performed crimes on them, the state may also place them (the victims) in prison as criminals and/ or seize their possessions, goods, and services. Along with that, any current goods or services linked to these individuals are also curtailed. Because of the high rate of recidivism, future decreases in money and/ or its value are also basically guaranteed.

From an economic standpoint, prisons must be made less costly, admit fewer persons, become economically sustainable, and/ or result in less recidivism. Wealthy nations can be made poor when they destroy their own money. Not only that, even free nations can become enslaved when goods and services are seized and destroyed to support any institution, including prisons. As such, prisons must not be seen as the first option to address crime, but rather the last option.

Chapter 23 (Part 2): The Destruction of Money – Prisons – Relevant Quotes (Quotes from other authors are excluded from the copyright of this book.)

"In the federal system alone, there were 90,000 prisoners locked up for drug offenses, compared with about 40,000 for violent crimes. A federal prisoner costs at least $30,000 a year to incarcerate, and females actually cost more." — Piper Kerman (Orange Is the New Black)

"The fee to cover the average cost of incarceration for Federal inmates was $34,704.12 ($94.82 per day) in FY 2016." — Federal Bureau of Prisons

"Finally, we spend lots of money. Spending on jails and prisons by state and federal governments has risen from $6.9 billion in 1980 to nearly $80 billion today. Private prison builders and prison service companies have spent millions of dollars to persuade state and local governments to create new crimes, impose harsher sentences, and keep more people locked up so that they can earn more profits. Private profit has corrupted incentives to improve public safety, reduce the costs of mass incarceration, and most significantly, promote rehabilitation of the incarcerated." — Bryan Stevenson (Just Mercy: A Story of Justice and Redemption)

"Piecing together state and federal reports, it appears that half the correctional population in California consists of illegal aliens. According to a state report, there were fewer than two hundred thousand inmates in the entire California prison population, including mental hospitals, in 2009. That year, 102,795 illegal aliens were incarcerated in California, costing the state more than $1 billion a year." — Ann Coulter (Adios, America!: The Left's Plan to Turn Our Country into a Third World Hellhole)

"Could this approach to public health have something to do with the fact that the incarceration rate in Norway is 71/ 100,000, in the Netherlands 81/ 100,000, and the US 781/ 100,000, while the crime rate in those countries is much lower than in ours, and the cost of medical care about half? Seventy percent of prisoners in California spent time in foster care while growing up. The United States spends $ 84 billion per year to incarcerate people at approximately $ 44,000 per prisoner; the northern European countries a fraction of that amount. Instead, they invest in helping parents to raise their children in safe and predictable surroundings. Their academic test scores and crime rates seem to reflect the success of those investments." — Bessel A. van der Kolk (The Body Keeps the Score: Brain, Mind, and Body in the Healing of Trauma)

"More costly to America than its 'war on terrorism' and our unpaid 19-trillion dollar debt in 2016, is the hidden price tag of systematically dismembered, stolen and incarcerated families, and the human rights violations in America's multi-billion dollar failed Foster Care, Adoption and Prison industries." — Lori Carangelo (CHOSEN CHILDREN 2016: People as Commodities in America's Failed Multi-Billion Dollar Foster Care, Adoption and Prison Industries)

"Although it costs taxpayers more than twice as much to send an 18-year-old to prison as to university, politicians reap greater rewards from lobbyists and conservative voters for building cells than for building classrooms." — Mike Davis (Ecology of Fear: Los Angeles And The Imagination Of Disaster)

"It costs about the same to house a maximum-security young adult prisoner for a year as it does to send his law-abiding counterpart to Harvard." — Robert Martensen (A Life Worth Living: A Doctor's Reflections on Illness in a High-Tech Era)

Chapter 24 (Part 1): The Destruction of Money – Healthcare

Keeping people healthy is conducive to the production of goods and services of a society. But, that does not mean that all healthcare expenditures provide that benefit. While vaccination of thousands or millions of persons may avoid an expensive epidemic, the performance of some surgical procedures cost more than the vaccinations of many. From the standpoint of economics, there is no unlimited resource of assets (as expressed in money) for spending on every single patient.

Healthcare expenses do not always result in increased benefits as a whole. For example, one machine can cost millions of dollars and be used on very few people, while cheaper preventive medical interventions, positively affecting thousands of people, may be overlooked. As such, the cost of the former is offset by decreasing expenses for the latter.

A good deal of resources may be spent on treating a patient from a deadly infectious respiratory disease, but little resource is allocated on proper personal protective equipment (e.g., masks)for healthcare providers (e.g., nurses) to keep them from getting the same deadly infectious respiratory disease. In such a case, money is consumed in taking care of one while assets are not allocated to someone else (or others). This all entails the selective transference of rights of ownership over goods and services.

Healthcare concerns can even shut down the economy. In such cases, debt is incurred and assets are decreased. The inevitable result is inflation (discussed in an earlier chapter in this book).

The destruction of money related to healthcare is also aggravated by excessive bureaucracy (e.g., healthcare administration and governmental requirements). There is no value added with excessive bureaucracy that siphons resources to sustain itself without any corresponding increase in either goods or services. Bureaucracy is also responsible for having those with resources pay extra for those who have insufficient resources. This may be done through having a surcharge for treating the uninsured. Or, it can be done by increasing the cost someone with resources must pay for the same procedure. In essence, this is transference of ownership rights of one person over his/ her property to another person. The transference has extra costs. Those overseeing that transfer of ownership rights take some of it for themselves. That results in even higher costs for those who lose a portion of their money (ownership rights).

On top of that, a large legal system also drains money away from the actual provision of proper healthcare. Fear of legal repercussions, often very costly, increases the costs of record keeping (to protect one in cases of litigation), promotes additional testing (sometimes of marginal value), and even curtails the progress of medical science. The legal system may get richer, but the affected persons (past, present and future) may actually obtain poorer quality care at higher costs. In effect, ownership of goods and services related to healthcare may be directed to those who have nothing to do whatsoever with actual healthcare.

The legal system does not operate by itself in affecting money as it pertains to healthcare. Insurance also has a major role in the allocation of goods and services, and, therefore, money. Diagnosis may be rendered according to insurance provider instructions. The most effective treatment may be delayed or denied. But the healthcare insurance industry is also syphoning money away from actual healthcare without increasing the goods and services in healthcare.

Finally, healthcare for a profit has a major influence on healthcare goods and services. When the label 'medical' is added to a product's name, the cost of the product increases. This is particularly true for medicines. Salt, for example, is cheap; salt tablets, when prescribed for medical reasons, are not. Adding a high profit margin to the equation of pharmaceuticals only decreases the amount of money available for other healthcare goods and services. The high cost of pharmaceuticals also contributes to the corruption of medical practice. Medical treatment is often changed to make more patients or clients take certain medications resulting in greater profits for pharmaceutical companies. Even the criteria for certain illnesses may be changed so that more people fall under the umbrella of having to take prescribed medications. Unfortunately, because medications have side effects, additional medications are prescribed to treat these side effects. A vicious cycle results. People are not cured, but drawn deeper into a labyrinth that serves to destroy their money (ownership over themselves along with their goods and services). This cost is compounded when profit margins are needed to please investors, but also to pay for litigation for side-effects (which happen with just about any medication or medical procedure conceivable).

Chapter 24 (Part 2): The Destruction of Money – Healthcare – Relevant Quotes (Quotes from other authors are excluded from the copyright of this book.)

"This is the only industry where technology advances have increased costs instead of lowering them." — Steven Brill (America's Bitter Pill: Money, Politics, Backroom Deals, and the Fight to Fix Our Broken Healthcare System)

"Is it not striking that the cost of food and clothing has gone steadily downwards over the past fifty years, while the cost of healthcare and education has gone steadily upwards?" — Matt Ridley (The Evolution of Everything: How New Ideas Emerge)

"The cost spikes for the government programs that protected the elderly and the poor were even worse. Better medical care kept people alive longer, and that meant Medicare had to pay for more complicated and more expensive treatment during those prolonged lives." — Steven Brill (America's Bitter Pill: Money, Politics, Backroom Deals, and the Fight to Fix Our Broken Healthcare System)

"Spiraling healthcare costs are the expected result because greater revenues are built into the basic principles that drive the system." — William Davis (Undoctored: Why Health Care Has Failed You and How You Can Become Smarter Than Your Doctor)

"Medicare, which pays hospitals based on their costs, plus overhead and a small profit margin, for providing each service, would have paid about $825 for all three tests." — Steven Brill (America's Bitter Pill: Money, Politics, Backroom Deals, and the Fight to Fix Our Broken Healthcare System)

The FDA doesn't require the manufacturers' ads to compare a drug's efficacy with that of other drugs or treatments - prescription or over-the-counter – or to list a price. Jublia, a topical drug for toenail fungus approved in 2014, was advertised during the 2016 Super Bowl. A little bottle of the solution sells for between $550 and $650 and the full forty-eight-week course of treatment for all your toes costs over $20,000. But Jublia's cure rates are under 20 percent. Lamisil (terbinafine), a pill that does the same with a higher cure rate, costs under $20." — Elisabeth Rosenthal (An American Sickness: How Healthcare Became Big Business and How You Can Take It Back)

"Meanwhile, administrative costs are eating up 15-30 percent of all health-care spending in the United States. That's twice the rate of most other advanced nations. This money goes mainly into collecting money: doctors collect from hospitals and insurers, hospitals collect from insurers, insurers collect from companies or from policyholders. At some hospitals, billing clerks outnumber physicians. A third of nursing hours are devoted to documenting tests and procedures so insurers have proof." — Robert B. Reich (Beyond Outrage)

"Medtronic's overall cost of making its products was about 25 percent of what it sells them for, yielding an unusually high gross profit margin of about 75 percent." — Steven Brill (America's Bitter Pill: Money, Politics, Backroom Deals, and the Fight to Fix Our Broken Healthcare System)

"First noted by the economist William Baumol in the 1960s, this phenomenon, now known as 'Baumol's cost disease,' basically says that prices in labor-intensive sectors such as healthcare and education increase faster than prices in sectors where most of the work can be more extensively automated."

— Rutger Bregman (Utopia for Realists: How We Can Build the Ideal World)

Chapter 25 (Part 1): Government Expenditures – Domestic

The government does redistribute wealth. When it does so, it takes legal claim over that owned by person/ persons, takes possession to itself, and transfers part of that to another person/ other persons. The transference of money is actually the transference of the legal claim to goods and services from one entity to another entity. Since a government does not really produce wealth (but it can manufacture currency), what the government has to give has to be taken from someone else. The difference in what it takes and in what it gives to person/ persons provides the funds for the government to function. And what function may that be? One of its major functions is the taking from one, giving to another, and keeping some for itself. However, in the end, the government decides from whom to take, what to take, how much to take, how much to keep, what to give, and to whom to give. The net result can lead to a decrease in actual total wealth while appearing to increase that wealth. The reason for that is because governments tend to become self-serving. Everyone and everything are viewed by the government as belonging to the government unless it gracefully allows others to possess what they own or produce.

Chapter 25 (Part 2): Government Expenditures – Domestic – Relevant Quotes (Quotes from other authors are excluded from the copyright of this book.)

"People who will not turn a shovel full of dirt on the project nor contribute a pound of material, will collect more money from the United States than will the People who supply all the material and do all the work. This is the terrible thing about interest ...But here is the point: If the Nation can issue a dollar bond, it can issue a dollar bill. The element that makes the bond good makes the bill good also. The difference between the bond and the bill is that the bond lets the money broker collect twice the amount of the bond and an additional 20%, whereas the currency, the honest sort provided by the Constitution, pays nobody but those who contribute in some useful way. It is absurd to say our Country can issue bonds and cannot issue currency. Both are promises to pay, but one fattens the usurer and the other helps the People. If the currency issued by the People were no good, then the bonds would be no good, either. It is a terrible situation when the Government, to insure the National Wealth, must go in debt and submit to ruinous interest charges at the hands of men who control the fictitious value of gold." — Thomas A. Edison

"America's abundance was created not by public sacrifices to the common good, but by the productive genius of free men who pursued their own personal interests and the making of their own private fortunes. They did not starve the people to pay for America's industrialization. They gave the people better jobs, higher wages, and cheaper goods with every new machine they invented, with every scientific discovery or technological advancement - and thus the whole country was moving forward and profiting, not suffering, every step of the way." — Ayn Rand

"In particular, the State has arrogated to itself a compulsory monopoly over police and military services, the provision of law, judicial decision-making, the mint and the power to create money, unused land ('the public domain'), streets and highways, rivers and coastal waters, and the means of delivering mail...the State relies on control of the levers of propaganda to persuade its subjects to obey or even exalt their rulers." — Murray N. Rothbard (The Ethics of Liberty)

"Higher government spending will not lead to more rapid monetary growth and inflation if additional spending is financed either by taxes or by borrowing from the public. In that case, government has more to spend, the public has less.

Higher government spending is matched by lower private spending for consumption and investment." — Milton Friedman (Free to Choose: A Personal Statement)

"Most officially 'poor' Americans today have things that middle-class Americans of an earlier time could only dream about - including color TV, videocassette recorders, microwave ovens, and their own cars. Moreover, half of all poor households have air-conditioning. Leftist redistribution of income could never accomplish that, because there are simply not enough rich people for their wealth to have such a dramatic effect on the living standards of the poor, even if it was all confiscated and redistributed. Moreover, many attempts at redistributing wealth in various countries around the world have ended up redistributing poverty. After all, rich people can see the political handwriting on the wall, and can often take their money and leave the country, long before a government program can get started to confiscate it. They are also likely to take with them skills and entrepreneurial experience that are even harder to replace than the money." — Thomas Sowell (Controversial Essays)

"The United States government continues to pour billions of dollars into research on cancer, while it also subsidizes the tobacco industry. Much of the research money goes toward animal experiments, many of them only remotely connected with fighting cancer - experimenters have been known to relabel their work 'cancer research' when they found they could get more money for it that way than under some other label." — Peter Singer (Animal Liberation: The Definitive Classic of the Animal Movement)

"There's no such thing as an entitlement because no one is entitled to anything. If you plan to live off of the generosity of your neighbors, it would behoove you to endear yourself to them so that they actually want to help you, because you do not have a right to anybody else's money. Nobody does. There isn't such a thing. We all have obligations but nobody in the Bible has a right to anything. The word doesn't exist in Hebrew because it doesn't exist in the world. When anyone coerces you to provide such a right, it is not charity by the very definition of charity, which is voluntary giving. If you are being coerced to give your money to someone, this is theft." — Daniel Lapin (Business Secrets from the Bible: Spiritual Success Strategies for Financial Abundance)

"Our politicians tell us we are free, even though most governments take over 50% of what we earn. They claim we get services that we need for our hard-earned money, even though we could buy the same services at half the price from the private sector. Today, we ridicule the slave-owners' claim that they 'gave back' to their slaves by housing, clothing, feeding them, and bestowing upon them the 'benefits' of civilization instead of leaving them in their native state. We see this as a self-serving justification for exploitation. In the future, we will view being forcibly taxed to pay for things we don't want, such as bombs for the Middle East, subsidies for tobacco, other people's abortions, regulations that put small businesses out of business, prisons for people trying to feel good, keeping life-saving medications out of the hands of dying people, etc., as taking away our freedom. When even a small portion of our lives is spent enslaved, that part tends to dominate the rest of our time. If we don't put our servitude first as we structure the remainder of our lives, our masters will make sure we regret it. How much freedom do we need to survive and how much do we need to thrive?" — Mary J. Ruwart

"There are many farm handouts; but let's call them what they really are: a form of legalized theft. Essentially, a congressman tells his farm constituency, 'Vote for me. I'll use my office to take another American's money and give it to you." — Walter E. Williams

"By deriving its just powers from the governed, government becomes primarily a mechanism for defense against bodily harm, theft, and involuntary servitude. It cannot claim the power to redistribute money or property nor to force reluctant citizens to perform acts of charity against their will. Government is created by the people. No individual possesses the power to take another's wealth or to force others to do good, so no government has the right to do such things either. The creature cannot exceed the creator." — Ezra Taft Benson (The Constitution: A Heavenly Banner) dying people, and is taking away our freedom. What does a small portion of our taxes [illegible] that part [illegible] the rest of our money. If we don't tell our servants [illegible] the [illegible] of our [illegible] (our masters) [illegible] make sure we [illegible] How much freedom do [illegible] give up and how much do we [illegible] — Mike [illegible]

[illegible] many [illegible] they really [illegible] congressman [illegible] vote for me [illegible]

[illegible]

Chapter 26 (Part 1): Government Expenditures – Foreign Aid

Money (legal claims to ownership over goods and services) can be transferred to a third party by the government. In cases of foreign aid, the monies given to a foreign country represent transference of a citizenry's rights to its goods and services to a foreign country. They are, as a matter of fact, being forced to supply their labor, their possessions, and even their future productivity to the service of another nation. If a nation's government gives a billion units (of whatever currency it has) to another nation, it is, in fact, taking a billion units, as per legal claim, from those it has taxed. Those taxed are in a sense serving two governments, the one which takes their money and the government to whom they have to provide goods/ services to satisfy the transfer of wealth by the first government. The citizens/ residents of the country that receive the foreign aid, in the meanwhile, do not have their rights to their goods and services diminished in the least.

Many of the actual costs of foreign aid are concealed. The presentation is that the transference of legal claims of ownership promotes/ stimulates the economy. That may be true if there was an increase in trade to offset the foreign aid. But, if the money only goes to a few people, trade does not increase with the country granting the aid. In fact, the country may simply choose to trade with an enemy/ competitor of its benefactor, thereby further decreasing the wealth of the donor nation. The money can also increase the wealth of just few persons who help only themselves. What may not be obvious is that to obtain the wealth to be given away as money, the people of the nation being taxed may suffer considerably. Their loss of legal claim over their possessions can lead to such things as increased poverty, loss of property, and fewer markets to sell their goods. A handshake of two smiling presidents, for example, can come at the cost of someone in the donor country losing his/ her home. And, the cost of lifting someone out of poverty in the recipient country can be pushing someone into poverty in the donor country.

Chapter 26 (Part 2): Government Expenditures – Foreign Aid – Relevant Quotes (Quotes from other authors are excluded from the copyright of this book.)

"The budget should be balanced, the Treasury should be refilled, public debt should be reduced, the arrogance of officialdom should be tempered and controlled, and the assistance to foreign lands should be curtailed, lest Rome become bankrupt. People must again learn to work, instead of living on public assistance." — Taylor Caldwell

"Our gain from foreign trade is what we import. Exports are the price we pay to get imports. As Adam Smith saw so clearly, the citizens of a nation benefit from getting as large a volume of imports as possible in return for its exports, or equivalently, from exporting as little as possible to pay for its imports." — Milton Friedman (Free to Choose: A Personal Statement)

"A majority of people in these surveys also said that America gives too much aid--but when they were asked how much America should give, the median answers ranged from 5 percent to 10 percent of government spending. In other words, people wanted foreign aid 'cut' to an amount five to ten times greater than the United States actually gives!" — Peter Singer (The Life You Can Save: Acting Now to End World Poverty)

"There are two important lessons here. First, foreign aid is not a very effective means of dealing with the failure of nations around the world today. Far from it. Countries need inclusive economic and political institutions to break out of the cycle of poverty." — Daron Acemoğlu (Why Nations Fail: The Origins of Power, Prosperity and Poverty)

"The great bulk of Marshall Plan funds returned to the United States, or never left, being paid directly to American corporations to purchase American goods. The US Agency for International Development (AID) stated in 1999: 'The principal beneficiary of America's foreign assistance programs has always been the United States.'" — William Blum (America's Deadliest Export)

"While some foreign charities are frauds, all government foreign aid programs are frauds because if we don't like how our money is being spent, we only have two choices: pay our taxes or go to jail." — Adam Kokesh (FREEDOM!)

"In 2004, the British envoy to Kenya, Sir Edward Clay, complained about rampant corruption in the country, commenting that Kenya's corrupt ministers were 'eating like gluttons' and vomiting on the shoes of the foreign donors." — Dambisa Moyo (Dead Aid: Why Aid Is Not Working and How There Is a Better Way for Africa)

"Putting an end to foreign aid is impractical and would likely lead to additional human suffering. It is impractical because citizens of many Western nations feel guilt and unease about the economic and humanitarian disasters around the world, and foreign aid makes them believe that something is being done to combat the problems. Even if this something is not very effective, their desire for doing it will continue, and so will foreign aid." — Daron Acemoğlu (Why Nations Fail: The Origins of Power, Prosperity, and Poverty)

Chapter 27 (Part 1): Government And Its Liquidity

Government claims to own everything, including people, things, labor, and services. Even what is given by nature/ God is claimed to be owned by the government, including the sun and the rain. And what it owns, it can manipulate, tax, limit, appropriate, and seize. As such, everything within a nation's borders and everything owned by its people (possibly anywhere in the world) can be placed under a claim of ownership by the government. As noted earlier, money is a legal claim of ownership to goods and services. And, due to the role of government in ownership, all money belongs to the government. Economic transactions become transference of what the government can ultimately control, seize, allocate, or destroy.

This is important in terms of how a government maintains its financial liquidity. The important thing to a government is its own financial liquidity. The financial liquidity of the people under its jurisdiction is only important in so far as it impacts the financial liquidity of government. When wealth is overtaxed, the possible seizable wealth also decreases. When too much wealth is seized by a foreign government, there will be a decline on what can be seized in the future. After all, even if that which belongs to a country's citizens overseas can be taxed or seized, that can only be done to the extent that the foreign nation permits it.

A government sustains its financial liquidity by reducing the financial liquidity (represented in monetary ownership) of those it levies taxes on. Such invariably leads to unequal taxation as those in power favor taxes that benefit their ownership claims or of those constituents who support the governing powers. Taxation, as such, can destroy segments of society by transferring the rights of ownership to their goods/ services to those whom the tax laws favor. Hence, taxation and debt involve, not only the power to destroy but also, the power to enslave its current people and their descendants. Yes, a country can spend itself into poverty. A country can tax and collect debt to the point that its sovereignty is lost. The tax diminishes the ability of the citizenry to pay off a debt. The debt itself transfers ownership of the country to a domestic or foreign entity. A democratic country can cease to be a democracy because of over burdensome debt and the consequences of such debt. Truly, debt can conquer a nation just as surely as military might.

Chapter 27 (Part 2): Government And Its Liquidity – Relevant Quotes (Quotes from other authors are excluded from the copyright of this book.)

"I discovered, for the first time but not the last, that politicians don't care too much what things cost. It's not their money." — Donald J. Trump (Trump: The Art of the Deal)

"It is a popular delusion that the government wastes vast amounts of money through inefficiency and sloth. Enormous effort and elaborate planning are required to waste this much money." — P.J. O'Rourke (Parliament of Whores: A Lone Humorist Attempts to Explain the Entire U.S. Government)

"Most of the energy of political work is devoted to correcting the effects of mismanagement of government." — Milton Friedman

"I cannot undertake to lay my finger on that article of the Constitution which granted a right to Congress of expending, on objects of benevolence, the money of their constituents." — James Madison

"A major source of objection to a free economy is precisely that it ... gives people what they want instead of what a particular group thinks they ought to want. Underlying most arguments against the free market is a lack of belief in freedom itself." — Milton Friedman

"And to preserve their independence, we must not let our rulers load us with perpetual debt. We must make our election between economy and liberty, or profusion and servitude. If we run into such debts, as that we must be taxed in our meat and in our drink, in our necessaries and our comforts, in our labors and our amusements, for our callings and our creeds, as the people of England are, our people, like them, must come to labor sixteen hours in the twenty-four, give the earnings of fifteen of these to the government for their debts and daily expenses; and the sixteenth being insufficient to afford us bread, we must live, as they now do, on oatmeal and potatoes; have no time to think, no means of calling the mismanagers to account; but be glad to obtain subsistence by hiring ourselves to rivet their chains on the necks of our fellow-sufferers." — Thomas Jefferson (Letters of Thomas Jefferson)

"Our minds tell us, and history confirms, that the great threat to freedom is the concentration of power. Government is necessary to preserve our freedom; it is an instrument through which we can exercise our freedom; yet by concentrating power in political hands, it is also a threat to freedom. Even though the men who wield this power initially be of good will and even though they be not corrupted by the power they exercise, the power will both attract and form men of a different stamp." — Milton Friedman

"It is with government, as Caesar said it was in war, that money and soldiers mutually supported each other; that with money he could hire soldiers, and with soldiers extort money." — Lysander Spooner (No Treason: The Constitution of No Authority)

"So far as we know, no pollster has asked the public, "Are you getting your money's worth for the more than 40 percent of your income being spent on your behalf by government?" — Milton Friedman (Free to Choose: A Personal Statement)

"We had to struggle with the old enemies of peace - business and financial monopoly, speculation, reckless banking, class antagonism, sectionalism, war profiteering. They had begun to consider the Government of the United States as a mere appendage to their own affairs. We know now that Government by organized money is just as dangerous as Government by organized mob." — Franklin D. Roosevelt

"A common objection to totalitarian societies is that they regard the end as justifying the means. Taken literally, this objection is clearly illogical. If the end does not justify the means, what does? But this easy answer does not dispose of the objection; it simply shows that the objection is not well put. To deny that the end justifies the means is indirectly to assert that the end in question is not the ultimate end, that the ultimate end is itself the use of the proper means. Desirable or not, any end that can be attained only by the use of bad means must give way to the more basic end of the use of acceptable means." — Milton Friedman (Capitalism and Freedom)

"If any man's money can be taken by a so-called government, without his own personal consent, all his other rights are taken with it; for with his money, the government can, and will, hire soldiers to stand over him, compel him to submit to its arbitrary will, and kill him if he resists." — Lysander Spooner

"Government actions often provide substantial benefits to a few while imposing small costs on many." — Milton Friedman (Why Government Is the Problem)

"Government always finds a need for whatever money it gets." — Ronald Reagan

"The government solution to a problem is usually as bad as the problem." — Milton Friedman

"It's clearly a budget. It's got lots of numbers in it." — George W. Bush

"If you have been voting for politicians who promise to give you goodies at someone else's expense, then you have no right to complain when they take your money and give it to someone else, including themselves." — Thomas Sowell

Chapter 28 (Part 1): National Debt And Future Generations

The power to enslave is particularly insidious when it comes to future generations whose rights to their goods/ services are seized, and therefore, their lives/ livelihoods, possibly before they are even born. They will not have the luxury of spending for perishable things as was done in the past. As such, debt ensures the decay of future freedoms along with the loss of current ones. Moreover, the ability of much of one generation to pass on accumulated wealth to the next generation diminishes. Consequently, the standard of living will decrease for the masses from which goods/ services are taken. But, it will not diminish the wealth of everyone in a society. A small minority will face increased wealth in the short term. But, without a sound basis for the whole of society to sustain the goods and services necessary to support the monetary claims of ownership, eventually even the standard of living of the affluent will diminish. Note: Feudal/ oligarchic societies have not been known, now or in the past, as having robust, rich economies.

Chapter 28 (Part 2): National Debt And Future Generations – Relevant Quotes (Quotes from other authors are excluded from the copyright of this book.)

"Money is like manure; it's only good if you spread it around." — Francis Bacon (The Essays)

"The principle of spending money to be paid by posterity, under the name of funding, is but swindling futurity on a large scale." — Thomas Jefferson

"A national debt, if it is not excessive, will be to us a national blessing." — Alexander Hamilton

"There are two ways to conquer and enslave a nation. One is by the sword. The other is by debt." — John G. Adams

"When a government is dependent upon bankers for money, they and not the leaders of the government control the situation, since the hand that gives is above the hand that takes. Money has no motherland; financiers are without patriotism and without decency; their sole object is gain." — Napoléon Bonaparte

"You can tell a lot about a country which refers to the Royal Mint and the National Debt." — William Cobbett

"One dollar at compound interest, at twenty-four per cent, for one hundred years, would produce a sum equal to our national debt. Interest eats night and day, and the more it eats the hungrier it grows. The farmer in debt, lying awake at night, can, if he listens, hear it gnaw. If he owes nothing, he can hear his corn grow. Get out of debt as soon as you possibly can. You have supported idle avarice and lazy economy long enough." — Robert G. Ingersoll (The Works of Robert G. Ingersoll, Vol. 1 [of 12] Dresden Edition-Lectures)

"Blessed are the young, for they shall inherit the national debt." — Herbert Hoover

"It is true that liberty is not free, nor is it easy. But tyranny - even varying degrees of it - is much more difficult, and much more expensive. The time has come to rein in the federal government, put it on a crash diet, and let the people keep their money and their liberty." — Ron Paul

"The national debt - that is, the unfunded liabilities and fiscal operating debt - amounts to tens of trillions of dollars. The Government Accountability Office, the Congressional Budget Office, and numerous other public and private institutions have sounded warning alarms about the oncoming crash. But no serious or effective steps have been taken to address this simmering financial and economic implosion." — Mark R. Levin (Plunder and Deceit: Big Government's Exploitation of Young People and the Future)

"We do not inherit the Earth from our ancestors, we borrow it from our children" — American proverb

Chapter 29 (Part 1): Control Of Money

At the beginning of this book, money was defined as being "a legal claim of ownership over the goods and services of a person or a people. People, who exchange money, sell it or purchase it, are involved in the acquisition of ownership rights of the goods or services of a person or people." As such, those who control money exert control over the goods and services of a person or a people. When one considers that control is the power over something (to be able to run it), then control of money means that one has power over money. By having control over money, one can make money, that legal claim of ownership, to do according to what one desires. But, when someone else controls your money, then that person/ entity makes money do according to what that he/ she wants it to do. And, that may not be always in one's best interest. It may also prove to be risky. First, the person/ entity who controls the money extracts some of the original portion to his/ her/ their gain. Second, if that person/ entity loses the money, such as from bankruptcy or litigation, one's money can also be lost. Third, there is an opportunity cost associated with control of one's money by someone else. The money is not available when one needs it. Fourth, the money may be simply applied to uses that are not necessarily in one's best interests or in accordance with one's beliefs.

Yielding control of one's money to another person/ entity means that one yields control over all or part of one's life, livelihood, destiny, and freedom to the other person/ entity. The other person/ entity who controls one's money now has a definitive say in what one's legal claim of ownership can or cannot do. To put it bluntly, whoever controls one's money controls him/ her. Perhaps that is why one of the first lessons that should be taught in finance at business schools is that one should control one's money. When business owners no longer control the business' money, they no longer control the business. How to actually control one's money is actually the subject addressed in many lengthy books and is a core issue in accounting, economics and finance. That, of course, is a topic far too detailed and lengthy for this book. The purpose of this book has been to define money, indicate what it does, and touch upon why one should control money (rather than be controlled by money).

Chapter 29 (Part 1): Control Of Money – Relevant Quotes (Quotes from other

authors are excluded from the copyright of this book.)

"If money is your hope for independence, you will never have it. The only real security that a man can have in this world is a reserve of knowledge, experience and ability." — Henry Ford

"Money is only a tool. It will take you wherever you wish, but it will not replace you as the driver." — Ayn Rand (Atlas Shrugged)

"Balancing your money is the key to having enough." — Elizabeth Warren

"You must gain control over your money or the lack of it will forever control you." — Dave Ramsey

"Once you deposit that money in your checking account, it becomes the bank's money and you're just another one of their creditors." — Kenneth Eade (Terror on Wall Street, a Financial Metafiction Novel)

Chapter 30 (Part 1): The Importance Of Prioritizing And Budgeting

There is no infinite supply of money. There are only so many goods and services to which legal claims of ownership can be made. Even if one were to forecast all needs/wants and have all future monies, there still is not enough money to satisfy every need or want.

Knowing that money is limited and that money is a legal claim of ownership, one has to prioritize how to utilize one's money. If one does not do so, then the shortage of money will definitely cause others to set their priorities regarding money upon that person. Remember that whoever controls money controls whatever money controls. As such, if one's money is controlled by someone else, it is no longer your money and that money can be used to control you.

Prioritizing and budgeting money also helps one to not become subservient to another who would control one's goods and services or, to put it more bluntly, control one's life. That means that one has to prioritize the use of money to that which does the most good without surrendering one's life and future doing so. Slavery is a high price for selecting the wrong priorities. Also, when one becomes enslaved, one no longer has control over who he/ she is, what he/ she can do, or what he/ she will be.

Money can be a useful ally when it is used properly and to its optimum utility/ efficiency. Money can be a cruel master when it is misappropriated. As such, a key component of prioritizing and budgeting is to ensure that one keeps control over his/ her own money and does not surrender it to someone else. Do not believe that those in government, business, charity organizations, or even religious institutions want to use your money for your benefit. They want to use your money to their benefit, regardless of the impact that it has on you, your life, your loved ones, or even your descendants. If you do not control your own money, you will be controlled.

How to prioritize and budget money is the subject of many texts. This book addressed what money is, what it does, and the need to control it; otherwise, one will be controlled by it. The authors of this text recommend continuous and serious study of money, particularly one's own, so that one can become free or remain free from the challenges it imposes.

Chapter 30 (Part 2): The Importance Of Prioritizing And Budgeting – Relevant Quotes (Quotes from other authors are excluded from the copyright of this book.)

"If you wish to make Pythocles rich, do not add to his store of money, but subtract from his desires." — Epicurus

"First, have a definite, clear practical ideal; a goal, an objective. Second, have the necessary means to achieve your ends: wisdom, money, materials, and methods. Third, adjust all your means to that end." — Aristotle

"A Penny Saved is a Penny Earned." — Benjamin Franklin

"The less you eat, drink, buy books, go to the theatre or to balls, or to the pub, and the less you think, love, theorize, sing, paint, fence, etc., the more you will be able to save and the greater will become your treasure which neither moth nor rust will corrupt - your capital. The less you are, the less you express your life, the more you have, the greater is your alienated life and the greater is the saving of your alienated being." — Karl Marx (Economic & Philosophic Manuscripts of 1844)

"We have become ninety-nine percent money mad. The method of living at home modestly and within our income, laying a little by systematically for the proverbial rainy day which is due to come, can almost be listed among the lost arts." — George Washington Carver

"The world says: 'You have needs -- satisfy them. You have as much right as the rich and the mighty. Don't hesitate to satisfy your needs; indeed, expand your needs and demand more.' This is the worldly doctrine of today. And they believe that this is freedom. The result for the rich is isolation and suicide, for the poor, envy and murder." — Fyodor Dostoyevsky (The Brothers Karamazov)

"The quickest way to double your money is to fold it in half and put it in your back pocket." – Will Rogers

"Fix in your mind the exact amount of money you desire. It is not sufficient merely to say, 'I want plenty of money.' Be definite as to the amount. 2. Determine exactly what you intend to give in return for the money you desire. (There is no such reality as 'something for nothing.') 3. Establish a definite date when you intend to possess the money you desire. 4. Create a definite plan for carrying out your desire, and begin at once, whether you are ready or not, to put this plan into action. 5. Write out a clear, concise statement of the amount of money you intend to acquire. Name the time limit for its acquisition. State what you intend to give in return for the money, and describe clearly the plan through which you intend to accumulate it. 6. Read your written statement aloud, twice daily, once just before retiring at night, and once after rising in the morning." — Napoleon Hill (Think and Grow Rich)

"Make your financial well-being a priority and stop spending on nonessential items. According to Webster's Dictionary, essential means: absolutely necessary; indispensable; vital. What definition are you using? Is your definition keeping you in financial bondage?" — Tiffany 'The Budgetnista' Aliche (The One Week Budget: Learn to Create Your Money Management System in 7 Days or Less!)

"If you don't budget when you have something, your creditors will do it for you when you have nothing." – James L. Jordan and Deovina N. Jordan daily once and before retiring at night and once after rising in the morning." — Napoleon Hill (Think and Grow Rich)

"Make your financial wellbeing a priority and stop sacrificing your financial dream [illegible] according to [illegible] everyone's [illegible]. [illegible] essential [illegible] necessary [illegible] independence [illegible]. What definition are you using? Is your definition keeping you in financial bondage?" — Tiffany "the Budgetnista" Aliche (The One Week Budget: Learn to Create Your Money [illegible] Automated [illegible])

[illegible]

Chapter 31 (Part 1): Not All Demands For Money Need To Be Honored

The world is full of people who want money. In fact, there is much more demand for money than the supply of money. On top of that, there is a greater demand for money than the intent to earn it. After all, people are often not only greedy; they also tend to be lazy.

It is easier to ask for a handout than to work for money. As such, the world abounds with people who demand money for their particular interests. They may use intimidation to get money. Or, they might use guilt or shame to increase their wealth. The important thing is that they want ownership of other people's goods and services, not for the benefit of the person who owns the goods and services but, for their own purposes.

That demand may be in the form of a request for a donation/ contribution. Or, it can be in the name of tithing. Regardless of the form of the demand, the message is that someone or something else is more deserving of what you possess than you are. In other words, you are being told to surrender part of your life, or control over your life, to someone else.

In spite of wanting to help, one can never have enough to help everyone (according to their desires) or to support every cause. In fact, even if one tried to do so, much of what one would allocate to another would never come close to doing what the money was apportioned for. When a demand for money is met, a demand for additional money follows. One ends up digging a hole to give away soil, only to be asked to dig a deeper hole for more soil. And that monetary hole ends up becoming the grave for one's economic health and personal freedom.

On top of that, many demands are contradictory to each other or do not share the same degree of importance to the donor or contributor. Ultimately, the donor has to prioritize the demands that others have regarding his/ her money. And, those priorities differ among persons. When the ability to prioritize changes from being voluntary to mandatory, then the donor also loses an essential component of being human, namely, having a free will over oneself and one's decisions, one's thoughts, one's activities, and one's possessions.

Chapter 31 (Part 2): Not All Demands For Money Need To Be Honored –

Relevant Quotes (Quotes from other authors are excluded from the copyright of this book.)

“The art of holding on to money is all about saying no to consumer culture.” — Austin Kleon (Steal Like an Artist: 10 Things Nobody Told You About Being Creative)

“Don’t go around saying the world owes you a living. The world owes you nothing. It was here first.” — Mark Twain

“It is not fair to ask of others what you are not willing to do yourself.” — Eleanor Roosevelt

“Be realistic, demand the impossible!” — Ernesto Che Guevara

“The basic question is not how much of our money we should give to God, but how much of God’s money we should keep for ourselves.” — Jim George (A Husband After God’s Own Heart)

“Don't give your money to the church. They should be giving their money to you.” — George Carlin

“The intercom buzzes while you’re changing your shirt. You push the Talk button: “Who is it?” “Narcotics squad. We’re soliciting donations for children all over the world who have no drugs." — Jay McInerney (Bright Lights, Big City)

"The difference between successful people and really successful people is that really successful people say no to almost everything." — Warren Buffett

"Those who give all they have to the poor end up joining the poor. Even giving must be budgeted." — James L. Jordan and Deovina N. Jordan

"Those who try to please everyone end up not even pleasing themselves or anyone." — James L. Jordan and Deovina N. Jordan

Chapter 32 (Part 1): There's More To Life Than Money

The quest for greater wealth can never be satiated. There is always something more that appeals to greed. And money induces greed like nothing else, for money also tempts with promises of power and glory. As such, it is with money that people sell their lives and their souls. They die for money that they never can spend. After all, the dead spend nothing and own nothing.

Being rich does not guarantee happiness. Even the rich suffer from depression. Even the rich commit suicide. And, even the rich die. What does a person ultimately show for his/ her life? Is it a bank account? No, that is left to others who are living. Is it property? No, that is also left to others who are still living. What we leave in the world is our impact on others. What we gain from life is how we lived and the quality of the life that we lived. It is true that much attention is given to those in the world who have lots of money. People listen to them as if they are particularly wise or knowledgeable. But that does not last.

Many of those whose words endure over the centuries, even through millennia, were not rich during their lifetimes.

Ultimately, life is for living. Life's true treasure is to appreciate life as the gift given to one by God. Life gives an opportunity to see beauty, to love, to be free, and to learn. All these can be lost if money becomes one's purpose for living. As Jesus Christ said almost two millennia ago, "No one can serve two masters. Either you will hate the one and love the other, or you will be devoted to the one and despise the other. You cannot serve both God and money" (Matthew 6:24). Serving God means one will end up serving humanity and that one can achieve true freedom, peace, and happiness. Serving money means that one will become enslaved to those who want to dominate/ control humanity and one will never find freedom, peace, and happiness.

Chapter 32 (Part 2): There's More To Life Than Money – Relevant Quotes (Quotes from other authors are excluded from the copyright of this book.)

“For this life is one of first fruits, not of tithes.” — Martin Luther (Luther’s Works, Volume 5 [Genesis Chapters 26-30])

“All the money in the world cannot pay for a life.” — Sylvain Reynard (Gabriel’s Inferno, #1)

“Money can’t buy you life.” — Bob Marley

“Happiness is not in the mere possession of money; it lies in the joy of achievement, in the thrill of creative effort.” — Franklin D. Roosevelt

“How you spend your time is more important than how you spend your money. Money mistakes can be corrected, but time is gone forever.” — David Norris

“Wealth File
1. Rich people believe ‘I create my life.’ Poor people believe ‘Life happens to me.’
2. Rich people play the money game to win. Poor people play the money game to not lose.
3. Rich people are committed to being rich. Poor people want to be rich.
4. Rich people think big. Poor people think small.
5. Rich people focus on opportunities. Poor people focus on obstacles.
6. Rich people admire other rich and successful people. Poor people resent rich and successful people.
7. Rich people associate with positive, successful people. Poor people associate with negative or unsuccessful people.

8. Rich people are willing to promote themselves and their value. Poor people think negatively about selling and promotion.
9. Rich people are bigger than their problems. Poor people are smaller than their problems.
10. Rich people are excellent receivers. Poor people are poor receivers.
11. Rich people choose to get paid based on results. Poor people choose to get paid based on time.
12. Rich people think 'both.' Poor people think 'either/ or.'
13. Rich people focus on their net worth. Poor people focus on their working income.
14. Rich people manage their money well. Poor people mismanage their money well.
15. Rich people have their money work hard for them. Poor people work hard for their money.
16. Rich people act in spite of fear. Poor people let fear stop them.
17. Rich people constantly learn and grow. Poor people think they already know." — T. Harv Eker (Secrets of the Millionaire Mind: Mastering the Inner Game of Wealth)

"The Dalai Lama, when asked what surprised him most about humanity, answered 'Man! Because he sacrifices his health in order to make money. Then he sacrifices money to recuperate his health. And then he is so anxious about the future that he does not enjoy the present; the result being that he does not live in the present or the future; he lives as if he is never going to die, and then dies having never really lived." — Dalai Lama XIV

Appendix 1: Miscellaneous Quotes About Money -- (Quotes from other authors are excluded from the copyright of this book.)

"For the best return on your money, pour your purse into your head." — Benjamin Franklin

"History reports that the men who can manage men manage the men who can manage only things, and the men who can manage money manage all." — Will Durant (The Lessons of History)

"You can be young without money, but you can't be old without it." — Tennessee Williams

"There is only one class in the community that thinks more about money than the rich, and that is the poor." — Oscar Wilde

"There's nothing in the world so demoralizing as money." — Sophocles (Antigone, Translations from Greek Drama)

"Lottery: A tax on people who are bad at math." — Ambrose Bierce (The Unabridged Devil's Dictionary)

"The lack of money is the root of all evil." — Mark Twain

"Money poisons you when you've got it, and starves you when you haven't." — D.H. Lawrence

"Always borrow money from a pessimist. He won't expect it back." — Oscar Wilde

"A rich man is nothing but a poor man with money." — W.C. Fields

"A Decalogue of Canons for Observation in Practical Life:
1. Never put off to tomorrow what you can do to-day.
2. Never trouble another with what you can do yourself.
3. Never spend your money before you have it.
4. Never buy a thing you do not want because it is cheap; it will be dear to you.
5. Take care of your cents: Dollars will take care of themselves.
6. Pride costs us more than hunger, thirst and cold.
7. We never repent of having ate too little.
8. Nothing is troublesome that one does willingly.
9. How much pain have cost us the evils which have never happened.

10. Take things always by their smooth handle.
11. Think as you please, and so let others, and you will have no disputes.
12. When angry, count to 10. Before you speak; if very angry, 100." — Thomas Jefferson (Letters of Thomas Jefferson)

"There's class warfare, all right, but it's my class, the rich class, that's making war, and we're winning." — Warren Buffett

"When it is a question of money, everybody is of the same religion. — Voltaire

"Money will not purchase happiness for the man who has no concept of what he wants." — Ayn Rand (Atlas Shrugged)

"Money can only give happiness where there is nothing else to give it." — Jane Austen (Sense and Sensibility)

"Rule No. 1: Never lose money. Rule No. 2: Never forget Rule No. 1." — Warren Buffett

"Religion is what keeps the poor from murdering the rich." — Napoléon Bonaparte

"[Credit is a system whereby] a person who can't pay, gets another person who can't pay, to guarantee that he can pay." — Charles Dickens (Little Dorrit)

"Money often costs too much." — Ralph Waldo Emerson

"America does not know the difference between money and sex. It treats sex like money because it treats sex as a medium of exchange, and it treats money like sex because it expects its money to get pregnant and reproduce." — Peter Kreeft (How to Win the Culture War: A Christian Battle Plan for a Society in Crisis)

"Only when the last tree has been cut down, the last fish been caught, and the last stream poisoned, will we realize we cannot eat money." — Cree Indian Prophecy

"A fool and his money are soon elected." — Will Rogers

"Money can't buy love, but it improves your bargaining position." — Christopher Marlowe

"Work like you don't need the money. Dance like no one is watching. And love like you've never been hurt." — Mark Twain

"All that we call human history--money, poverty, ambition, war, prostitution, classes, empires, slavery--[is] the long terrible story of man trying to find something other than God which will make him happy." — C.S. Lewis (Mere Christianity)

"Spending of the best part of one's life earning money in order to enjoy questionable liberty during the least valuable part of it, reminds me of the Englishman who went to India to make a fortune first, in order that he might return to England and live the life of a poet. He should have gone up the garret at once."

— Henry David Thoreau (Walden and Other Writings, Modern Library Classics)

"Money doesn't make us anyway; it just unmasks us." — Henry Ford

"Words are the counters of wise men, and the money of fools." — Thomas Hobbes

"So you think that money is the root of all evil. Have you ever asked what is the root of all money?" — Ayn Rand

"Remember, for every shot you fire, someone, somewhere, is making money." — Tom Clancy

"There are treasures in books that all the money in the world cannot buy, but the poorest laborer can have for nothing." — Robert G. Ingersoll

"Not, how much of my money will I give to God, but, how much of God's money will I keep for myself?" — John Wesley

"A real gentleman, even if he loses everything he owns, must show no emotion. Money must be so far beneath a gentleman that it is hardly worth troubling about." — Fyodor Dostoyevsky

"Poverty is not only a lack of money; it's a lack of sense of meaning." — David Bornstein (How to Change the World: Social Entrepreneurs and the Power of New Ideas)

“Yes, the truth is that men’s ambition and their desire to make money are among the most frequent causes of deliberate acts of injustice.” — Aristotle (Politics)

“Endless money forms the sinews of war.” — Marcus Tullius Cicero

“Get to know two things about a man. How he earns his money and how he spends it. You will then have the clue to his character. You will have a searchlight that shows up the inmost recesses of his soul. You know all you need to know about his standards, his motives, his driving desires, his real religion.” — Robert J. McCracken

“Money won’t create success, the freedom to make it will.” — Nelson Mandela

“Enjoying living was learning to get your money’s worth and knowing when you had it.” — Ernest Hemingway (The Sun Also Rises)

“Fidelity purchased with money, money can destroy.” — Seneca (The Conquest of Happiness)

“If you wish to get rich, save what you get. A fool can earn money; but it takes a wise man to save and dispose of it to his own advantage.” — Brigham Young

“The middle classes have a truly extraordinary conception of society. They really believe that human beings . . . have real existence only if they make money or help to make it.” —

Friedrich Engels (The Condition of the Working Class in England)

"Lack of money is the root of all evil." — George Bernard Shaw

"He that has the opinion money will do everything may well be suspected of doing everything for money." — Benjamin Franklin

"Money is a needful and precious thing, and when well used, a noble thing, but I never want you to think it is the first or only prize to strive for. I'd rather see you poor men's wives, if you were happy, beloved, contented, than queens on thrones, without self-respect and peace." — Louisa May Alcott

"KNOWLEDGE will not attract money, unless it is organized, and intelligently directed, through practical PLANS OF ACTION, to the DEFINITE END of accumulation of money. Lack of understanding of this fact has been the source of confusion to millions of people who falsely believe that 'knowledge is power.' It is nothing of the sort! Knowledge is only potential power. It becomes power only when, and if, it is organized into definite plans of action, and directed to a definite end." — Napoleon Hill (Think and Grow Rich [Illustrated & Annotated])

"We must magnetize our minds with intense DESIRE for riches, that we must become 'money conscious' until the DESIRE for money drives us to create definite plans for acquiring it." — Napoleon Hill (Think And Grow Rich)

“He who buys what he does not need steals from himself.” — Swedish Proverb

“Money grows on the tree of Persistence.” — Japanese Proverb

Appendix 2: Authors Of Quotes Cited In Book (Quotes from the following authors are excluded from the copyright of this book.):

Acemoglu, Daron: 1967-
Adams, John G.: 1735-1826
Ahamed, Liaquat: Late 19th century-1952
Alcott, Louisa May: 1832-1888
Aliche, Tiffany: 1979-
Amis, Martin: 1949-
Aristotle: 384-322 BC
Austen, Jane: 1775-1817
Bacon, Francis: 1561-1626
Behn, Aphra: 1640-1689
Benson, Ezra Taft: 1899-1994
Bierce, Ambrose: 1842-1914
Billings, Josh: 1818-1885
Bishop, Morris: 1893-1973
Blum, William: 1933-2018
Blyth, Mark: 1967-
Bonaparte, Napoleon: 1769-1821
Bornstein, David: 1940-
Bregman, Rutger: 1988-
Brill, Steven: 1950-
Brook, Yaron: 1961-
Brooks, John: 1920-1993
Bryan, William Jennings: 1860-1925
Buffett, Warren: 1930-

Burrough, Bryan: 1961-
Bush, George W.: 1946-
Caldwell, Taylor: 1900-1985
Carangelo, Lori: 1945-
Carlin, George: 1937-2008
Carver, George Washington: 1861/1864-1943
Clancy, Tom: 1947-
Chang, Ha-Joon: 1963-
Chodorov, Frank: 1887-1966
Cicero, Marcus Tullius: 106-43 BC
Cobbett, William: 1763-1835
Coulter, Ann Hart: 1961-
Dalai Lama XIV: 1935-
Davis, Mike: 1946-
Davis, William: 1957-
De Tocqueville, Alexis: 1805-1859
Dickens, Charles: 1812-1870
Dostoyevsky, Fyodor: 1821-1881
Durant, Will: 1885-1981
Eade, Kenneth: 1957-
Edison, Thomas A.: 1847-1931
Einstein, Albert: 1879-1955
Eisenhower, Dwight D.: 1890-1969
Eker, T. Harv: 1954-
Emerson, Ralph Waldo: 1803-1882
Engels, Friedrich: 1820-1895
Epicurus: 341-270 BC
Ferguson, Niall: 1964-
Fields, W. C.: 1880-1946
Fisher, Irving: 1867-1947
Ford, Henry: 1863-1947

Franklin, Benjamin: 1706-1790
Friedman, Milton: 1912-2006
Fukuyama, Francis: 1952-
George, Jim: 1943-
Graeber, David: 1961-2020
Greenspan, Alan: 1926-
Griffin, G. Edward: 1931-
Guevara, Ernesto Che: 1928-1967
Hamilton, Alexander: 1755-1804
Hazlitt, Henry: 1894-1993
Heath, Joseph: 1967 -
Heinlein, Robert A.: 1907-1988
Hemingway, Ernest: 1899-1961
Hess, Karl: 1923-1994
Hill, Napoleon: 1883-1970
Hobbes, Thomas: 1588-1679
Hoover, Herbert: 1874-1964
Hope, Bob: 1919-1998
Hudson, Michael: 1939-
Icke, David: 1952-
Ingersoll, Robert G: 1833-1899
Jefferson, Thomas: 1743-1826
John Fire Lame Deer: 1903-1976
Johnston, David Cay: 1948-
Judt, Tony: 1948-2010
Kant, Immanuel: 1724-1804
Kautilya: Lived during the third century BC
Kerman, Piper: 1969-
Keynes, John Maynard: 1883-1946
Kleon, Austin: 1983-
Klepper, Michael (Mike): 1934-

Kokesh, Adam: 1982-
Kreeft, Peter: 1937-
Lakoff, George Philip: 1941-
Laphan, Lewis Abbot: 1909-1995
Lapin, Daniel: 1947-
Lawrence, D.H.: 1885-1930
Lee, IIchi: 1950-
Lendman, Stephen: 1934-
Leno, Jay: 1950-
Levin, Mark: 1957-
Lewis, C.S.: 1898-1963
Lincoln, Abraham: 1809-1865
Luther, Martin: 1483-1546
MacLeod, Ken: 1954-
Madison, James: 1751-1836
Mandela, Nelson: 1918-2013
Marley, Roberg 'Bob' Nesta: 1945-1981
Marlow, Christopher: 1564-1593
Marmell, Ari: 1974-
Martensen, Robert: 1947-2013
Marx, Karl: 1818-1883
McCracken, Robert James: 1904-1973
McInerney, Jr., John Barrett (Jay): 1955-
Mill, John Stuart: 1806-1873
Morales, Carlos: 1969-
Molyneux, Stefan: 1966-
Moyo, Dambisa: 1969-
Nietzsche, Friedrich: 1844-1900
Obama, Barack: 1961-
O'Rourke, P.J.: 1947-
Orwell, George: 1903-1950

Paterson, Isabel: 1886-1961
Paul, Ron: 1935-
Perkins, John: 1945-
Piketty, Thomas: 1971-
Plato: 428/427 BC-348/347 BC
Pratchett, Terry: 1948-
Ramsey, Dave: 1960-
Rand, Ayn: 1905-1982
Reagan, Ronald: 1911-2004
Reich, Robert: 1946-
Reynard, Sylvain: 1950-
Ridley, Matthew (Matt) White: 1958-
Robin, Vicki: 1945-
Rogers, Will: 1879-1935
Roosevelt, Eleanor: 1884-1962
Roosevelt, Franklin D.: 1882-1945
Rosenthal, Elisabeth: 1956-
Rothbard, Murray Newton: 1926-1995
Ruwart, Mary J.: 1949-
Schroeder, Alice: 1956-
Scruton, Roger: 1944-2020
Seneca: 4 BC-65 AD
Shaw, George Bernard: 1856-1950
Singer, Peter: 1946-
Smith, Adam: 1723-1790
Sophocles: 496-406 BC
Sowell, Thomas: 1930-
Spooner, Lysander: 1808-1887
Stevenson, Bryan: 1959-
Stiglitz, Joseph Eugene: 1943-
Swift, Jonathan: 1667-1745

Their, Robert: 1988-
Thoreau, Henry David: 1817-1862
Thucydides: circa 460-404 BC
Tolkien, J.R.R.: 1892-1973
Tolstoy, Leo: 1828-1910
Trump, Donald J.: 1946-
Tucker, Jeffrey Albert: 1963-
Twain, Mark: 1835-1910
Tzu, Sun: Late sixth century BC
Van der Kolk, Bessel: 1943-
Vidal, Gore: 1925-2012
Voltaire: 1694-1778
Von Mises, Ludwig: 1881-1973
Warren, Elizabeth Ann: 1949-
Washington, George: 1732-1799
Wesley, John: 1703-1791
Wicksell, Knut: 1851-1926
Wilde, Oscar: 1854-1900
Williams, Tennessee: 1911-1983
Williams, Walter E.: 1936-
Wolf, Virginia: 1882-1941
Wouk, Herman: 1915-2019
Young, Brigham: 1801-1877

ABOUT THE AUTHORS

James L. Jordan, PhD, PhD, and Deovina N. Jordan, PhD, MD, celebrate more than 80 years of combined remarkable experiences in their professional lives. They are noted for their significant achievements and outstanding successes in science, management, healthcare, and higher education (with senior professorial ranks). Dr. James L. Jordan and Dr. Deovina N. Jordan have authored several books and many peer reviewed journal articles. They are developing scientific theories. Dr. James L. Jordan and Dr. Deovina N. Jordan have been highlighted in over 20 editions of Marquis Who's Who (in America, West, World, Education, Medicine, Healthcare, and Worldwide Lifetime Achievement).

Dr. James L. Jordan and Dr. Deovina N. Jordan live in their farm in the mountains with their two Yorkshire terriers and abundant wildlife. They share a love for wisdom literature and nature.

ABOUT THE BOOK

Everyone knows that money exists. However, many people don't know what it really is. For some, money is often regarded as something ethereal. For many, it is viewed as something one has in the bank, namely assets. Hence, at times, people consider it as the measure of a person's "worth." For much of humanity, money is the medium by which one purchases things or pays taxes (e.g., to a governmental body). In addition, money is often seen as being cash. As such, people ask "How much money do you have?" However, money is far more than an asset, a medium, cash, or other forms of financial transaction.

By not knowing what money truly is, or what money really does to people's lives, one has no real idea how to gain mastery over it. If money is considered as something out in the clouds, then it eludes being controlled. As such, money ends up controlling one in ways that persons and even organizations do not truly understand. Therefore, the truth about money must be told. Money must be defined. When one knows what money truly is, then one can understand its power and can free oneself from being its slave. The purpose of this book is to present a new perspective about money by introducing a new definition of money, indicating what it does and explaining why one should control his/ her money.

Jesus Christ told His followers, "The truth shall set you free." He also indicated that no one can serve two masters, money and God. Either one serves God and not money, or one serves money and not God. Therefore, to be able to truly serve God, one has to know money and what it does. In that way, one can live in a manner in which money is not one's master, but one's servant, thereby freeing one to serve God and not money.

To facilitate understanding of the concept of money, what money does, and how to gain mastery over money, the different chapters of this book are presented in two parts (Part 1 and Part 2). The first part features the concepts and theory being presented by the authors. The second part involves excerpts/ quotations made by different individuals that largely concur with the position being taken by the authors of this book. Ownership of the excerpts/ quotations of/ from other authors/ sources is not being claimed by this book's authors. The other authors/ sources are duly noted and their quotes are verifiable via the internet. Utilization of their quotes in Part 2 of the 32 chapters and in the Appendix is in accordance with fair use under the United States Copyright Law. As such, the quotes are included only to give support, via historical sources, of the original materials presented in Part 1 of the 32 chapters. The original materials are owned and copyrighted by the authors (James L. Jordan and Deovina N. Jordan) and has been registered as being so by the United States Copyright office.

This book is not about what form of money and how much money to save, or where and when to invest money, or even the differences among occupations (e.g., comparative worth). Such considerations can only take place when one understands what money truly is and what money actually does/ represents. Actual application of such knowledge is up to the individual according to his/ her opportunities, challenges, and economic, social, political, legal, and religious environments.

OTHER BOOKS WRITTEN BY THE AUTHORS

God: Answering the Mysteries of God, God's Existence, the Trinity, and God's Love; and How to Have a Personal Relationship with God

EBook link: **amazon.com/dp/B082RNRVBF**

The Universe is Not Dying: A unified physics theory explaining the mysteries of dimensions, space, strings, matter, energy, light, time, particle spin, wave formation, black holes, quasars, and the energy-matter cycle

EBook link: **amazon.com/dp/B083DP6MVC**

Drs. Jordan's Fables: Book One

Ebook link: **amazon.com/dp/B084FZH9DY**

Drs. Jordan's Fables: Book Two

EBook link: **amazon.com/dp/B084WNG8W8**

Thus Says The Lord God

EBook link: **amazon.com/dp/B085BLSH23**

Drs. Jordan's Fables: Book Three

EBook link: **amazon.com/dp/B085QBWXHP**

Thus Say The Biblical Prophets And Apostles: Volume I

EBook link: **amazon.com/dp/B08689G32J**

Thus Say The Biblical Prophets And Apostles: Volume II

EBook link: **amazon.com/dp/B086JFY6KB**

What Is A Good Husband?

EBook link: **amazon.com/dp/B0871T5ZQQ**

The Lost Books Of Wisdom

EBook link: **amazon.com/dp/B087BF3WV6**

The Ancient Wisdom Of The West

EBook link: **amazon.com/dp/B087Q566F7**

Christian Faith In The Age Of Disbelief And Unbelief: Attaining, Growing And Maintaining The Christian Faith Needed For Salvation

EBook link: a**mazon.com/dp/B0881J6LM3**

Drs. Jordan's Proverbial Wit And Wisdom From The Animal Kingdom

EBook link: **amazon.com/dp/B088F6RSQ7**

DRS. JORDAN's WHATS, WHYS and HOWS RATIONALES of CARDIOLOGY BOOK ONE: CARDIOVASCULAR SYSTEM

EBook link: **amazon.com/dp/B089GJH86C**

THE ANCIENT WISDOM OF THE STOICS: The Art Of Harnessing the Power Of Thought

EBook link: **amazon.com/dp/B08DMCQWHT**

Many peer reviewed journal articles

Please leave a review!

Dear Readers:

We thank you for reading our book. If you learned from it and enjoyed reading it, we would appreciate it very much if you could leave a review of our book at Amazon and GoodReads. Your review is extremely important. It gives us valuable feedback on what you like or did not like about our book. It will help us strengthen and improve our book. Moreover, it also helps other readers learn how to benefit from our book.

We appreciate your time and effort in writing your review of our book. We read all reviews enthusiastically. We are sure Amazon and GoodReads readers will, too!

Sincerely,

James L. Jordan, PhD, PhD and Deovina N. Jordan, PhD, MD

Made in United States
Orlando, FL
04 November 2026

90200301R00125